2019

NEVER
SETTLE

NEVER SETTLE

Sports, Family, and the
American Soul

MARTY SMITH

TWELVE

NEW YORK   BOSTON

Twelve
Hachette Book Group
1290 Avenue of the Americas, New York, NY 10104
twelvebooks.com
twitter.com/twelvebooks

First Edition: August 2019

Twelve is an imprint of Grand Central Publishing. The Twelve name and logo are trademarks of Hachette Book Group, Inc.

The publisher is not responsible for websites (or their content) that are not owned by the publisher.

The Hachette Speakers Bureau provides a wide range of authors for speaking events. To find out more, go to www.hachettespeakersbureau.com or call (866) 376-6591.

All photos courtesy of the author.

Library of Congress Cataloging-in-Publication Data
Names: Smith, Marty (Martin), 1976- author.
Title: Never settle: family, football, and tryin' to be better / Marty Smith.
Description: New York: Twelve, [2019]
Identifiers: LCCN 2019007493 | ISBN 9781538732991 (hardcover) | ISBN 9781549122538 (audio download) | ISBN 9781538733004 (ebook)
Subjects: LCSH: Smith, Marty (Martin), 1976- | Sportscasters—United States—Biography. | Television journalists—United States—Biography.
Classification: LCC GV742.42.S538 S65 2019 | DDC 070.449796092 [B]—dc23
LC record available at https://lccn.loc.gov/2019007493

ISBNs: 978-1-5387-3299-1 (hardcover), 978-1-5387-3300-4 (ebook),
978-1-5387-1726-4 (signed hardcover), 978-1-5387-1723-3 (B&N signed hardcover)

Printed in the United States of America

LSC-C

10 9 8 7 6 5 4 3 2 1

For the believers.
Most notably Lainie, Cambron, Mia, and Vivian.

Contents

Foreword

By Eric Church

There are two types of situations when lives change. One you recognize immediately and you know for certain, my life will never be the same. Second, and frankly more interesting, are those chance encounters that you don't immediately put into the life-changing category.

Those are my favorite to look back on.

I tell you that, to tell you this: My life changed one night on my bus outside of a club in North Carolina, in a mundane gravel parking lot, in which about two hundred crazy people had parked their vehicles and planned to drink and party and puke the night away.

My job? Provide the drink and the party.

But before I did that, in those days, I would have my meet-and-greet in the front lounge of my bus. Why? Good question. The short answer is: The clubs were so damn small you couldn't do it backstage.

There was no backstage. There was onstage, and in the crowd, that's it.

But I digress. Back to the meet-and-greet protocol: two or three at a time, single file, quick hello, what's your name, that's nice, smile for the camera. So imagine my surprise and intrigue when a skinny redhead—and I mean a coiffed redheaded fellow—stuck out his hand and, with an intense emotional story in his eyes, said, "Your record *Sinners Like Me* saved my life. I'm Marty Smith."

Bam! Little did I know that life had just changed forever.

No, that night we chatted about how music heals hurt and, in this case, how mine had healed his. I was touched but was oblivious to the future crop God had planted with the seeds of those words.

I don't remember the show; Marty does. I don't remember the place; Marty does. I don't even remember which city the place was in, but—you guessed it—Marty does.

What stuck with me was his intensity and passion and sincerity. He carried his story in a way I hadn't seen a story carried before.

This was thrust to the forefront of my mind a short time later when I was invited to join Marty on Percy Priest Lake in Nashville for a fishing derby to benefit a good cause. The cause? I don't remember, but ask Marty.

I immediately said yes, and then proceeded to arrive ten minutes late just because, well, I'm always late, and these things never start on time. Except these things, being fish derbies, actually do start on time. Emphatically, *do*.

They had a shotgun start. Clock strikes 8 a.m.! Bam! Two hundred bass boats race out at warp speed to slay their scaled nemesis at the far reaches of the lake's fingers.

So imagine my surprise and, truthfully, my amusement to pull up to a completely empty marina on tournament day.

All gone. Ghost town. Except for one lone boat, floating like a bobber on a backwoods catfish pond.

This lone vessel had two occupants. One had a mop of red hair spraying every which way. The other occupant, our fishing pro.

His name escapes me; ask Marty. So I walk down and sheepishly utter my apologies. Nameless fish pro looked less than amused.

Marty, on the other hand, looked incredibly amused.

So now we got a real problem, says fish guy: "All the other boats have a ten-minute head start, and they will have all the best spots staked out." I look around. Marty looks around. No one. Anywhere.

Marty says, "Let's fish around the marina here." Fish guy looks at Marty, takes about three deep breaths, looks to the sky, considers the epic waste of time this day (and probably his career choice) will be, takes an additional breath, looks back at Marty—because there is no way in hell he is gonna look at me—and says, "Why not? We are probably too late, anyway."

Short story long. We won. In a landslide.

My favorite moment of the whole thing was after we got the trophy, a country music peer of mine, who took everything too seriously, walked up in a huff and said, "We scoured dis whole gol-damn lake and caught nary a thing. Where da hell yous guys catch dem?"

I just turned around and pointed at the boat launch and said, "Right there." He was incredulous and, frankly, never the same professionally.

That day was the beginning of a thousand stories I could tell you. Stories of success, and recognition, and accolades, and world championships, and awards, and champagne, and beaches, and GOATS, and checkered flags, and pirate flags, and dammit moments so full of life you feel like you're flying.

Sometimes truthfully—flying on the gentle flowing 96 proof wings of Jack Daniel's. We damn sure were.

There were other times when we didn't fly. When we leaned on each other on the ground. Held each other up, overcome with loss, hurt, death.

I think back many nights to that show Marty knows, in that parking lot Marty knows, on that night Marty knows, in that city Marty knows, and I know only one thing, the most important thing.

He thinks my music saved him, but I know his friendship saved me.

Preface

Never *Settle* is like a record album. That was my entire philosophy toward its production, arrangement, and execution. It's an unorthodox approach for a book. It's different. But I've never been especially traditional.

Many books build, chapter upon chapter, toward a climax. It is a proven formula, centuries old. Meanwhile, great record albums tell a broader story through a collection of individual tracks, each with unique characters and diverse settings and great imagery that work together to share specific stories, which are often separate from the stories told by their sister tracks. One song can seemingly have no exact correlation to the next. The characters and their respective lessons are capable of standing alone. Just turn on the radio for proof.

But if done well, each individual track on an album blends with the others emotionally to create a thematic journey. Collectively, they wrap the listener in a comprehensive story. They might even shape a life, and often do. Like the songs on an album, each story within these pages can stand alone as a singular experience. But housed together, they collectively provide stops on a journey toward the goal for this book, which is the unyielding search for the American soul, and how sports provide a vehicle to find it.

The idea made sense. We love victory. That's the purpose for playing the games. But the stories, the souls, the community, and the journeys within the games are often what move us. They are the foundation upon which the games are built. They are the "why" and the "how" that provide context to the "who" and the "what" we cheer.

As an interviewer, I've been blessed with a rare luxury: breadth. Rather than focusing on one specific theme or moment during interviews, I often have freedom to inquire and learn about the "hows" and the "whys" of the interviewees' stories.

I consider us all pieces of clay. Every win, loss, acquaintance, relationship, and experience along the way pinches at that clay to remold us. Every individual we meet sculpts our evolving shape. Some soften our sharp edges. Some strengthen our weak foundations. Some take small pinches. Some take chunks. I love learning about those chunks, who took them, and how they reshaped our perspectives and redirected our paths.

Some of my greatest blessings are the editors, producers, and executives who believed in a brand of storytelling focused on the human element. I thoroughly enjoy the opportunity to introduce an audience to a side they may not have seen before of someone they admire. From the moment I left college and took my first reporting opportunity at the *Lynchburg News & Advance*, my bosses enabled me to learn a certain storytelling craft, long-form and detail-oriented, in real time. I cannot stress how rare that is, especially today, in a 280-character news world that can shift seismically in an instant. It did not come without mistakes. I've made plenty. Nearly every one of my bosses championed a philosophy that dug deeply into the "who" beneath the "what." And my bosses and colleagues at ESPN most certainly champion that approach. I am so grateful for all of you—including those who told me to my face it would never work.

Especially them.

They helped title this book. Their doubt provided an edge for me. Their doubt disallowed complacency and demanded account- ability. You will learn about my doubts and insecurities within these pages. I'm intense, but generally easygoing. And I'm com- petitive as hell. I pride myself on being a tireless workhorse. There are better reporters. But nobody will outwork me. No one will have more passion than I will. No one will have more joy than I will. I can control those variables: work ethic, passion, and joy.

"Never settle" has been a personal philosophy for many years now, as a husband, father, friend, brother, athlete, and profes- sional. I haven't always succeeded. But failure only motivated me to try harder and strive to be better. I want to give every ounce of everything within me while I'm here.

"Good enough" ain't good enough. My parents died young. I learned that pain early. And I decided then that I would live and love as hard as I could, in as many areas as I could find. Try new things. Take chances. Love hard. Play hard. Pray hard. Work hard. Listen. Be kind. Ask for forgiveness.

In *Never Settle*, you will read about lessons I learned from time spent with icons like Nick Saban and Tiger Woods. But you'll also read about my family, my mentors, and my roots. My wins and my losses. Those I've loved, many of whom are gone too soon but live on within me, good and bad. This book has the tendencies of a memoir. It is not a memoir. It's a chronicle of memorable moments that helped shape the man I am right now, a man in his early for- ties still trying every day to figure out what he's doing here and how he might do it better; a man who has seen the world but is forever rooted in rural America.

I wanted to include poetry within these pages, musings jotted down on cross-country flights over the years. I wanted to place stories and quotes from insightful interviews between chapters. So I did. Artists need great producers to adjust and mold their visions and their talents into their most powerful forms. I call that "making it a copyright." I am beyond appreciative that my friends at Twelve agreed to hold my hand on this journey, embrace a weird approach toward a common project, and make it better than I ever dreamed it could be. They let me achieve a dream.

Any record album worth its salt is vulnerable.

If nothing else, *Never Settle* is vulnerable. Not only because I have made myself vulnerable through the act of writing this book but because the subjects included herein made themselves vulnerable to me as they opened up to share intimate slices of their life journeys. As for me? I do not share all of my shortcomings or insecurities in this book, but I share a bunch of them. I've made plenty of mistakes. I've wandered from my faith at times, and for lengthy periods. I strive to be kind to everyone, but I have not always succeeded. When I have failed, I've sought forgiveness.

I have tried to live by the Golden Rule: to treat others as I'd like to be treated.

I don't know how long I'll make it here on this earth, and ultimately I want my children to have a piece of their daddy, a way to know me more deeply even after I'm gone. A way I never knew my daddy. Lainie and our kids have sacrificed so much for my career. They wonder aloud why Daddy has to leave again and why he's on airplanes all the time. I hope that this book can help answer some of those questions when they're older. And I hope it makes you consider your own hopes and desires for your own life.

I've long told my friends in music how envious I am that they create art that lives forever. "Copyrights." With *Never Settle*, maybe we've done that.

I have experienced moments of euphoria and moments of great sorrow. I'm a dad and a husband who grew from an immature, egocentric person into something of an accountable man. Maybe some of you will relate.

The great albums are just that: relatable. I hope this one is, too.

Chapter One

Jump!

Jumping off the boathouse roof was Nick Saban's idea.

Saban's boathouse, on the banks of Lake Burton, Georgia, is a gorgeous structure. It is two stories, the bottom made of ornate stone and staggered wood shakes, providing a covered two-boat garage of sorts for his watercraft. One stall held a pontoon boat and the other a stunning antique cherrywood cruiser, with real glass and gold trim and Old Glory waving off the back. It looked like art.

Atop all of this sat a flawless wood-floor landing with an unimpeded lake view, surrounded by a wrought-iron fence, the back half of which included a pavilion in which to dine and evade the sun. Up the hill and a rock walkway sat the lake house.

It was early afternoon, late August, and Saban, Tim Tebow, and I stood at the edge of the second-floor wooden platform, overlooking the water below. During some small talk, Saban said we should jump.

The moment was spontaneous but hinted at a dare.

"I do it all the time, boys. Sack up."

One of those deals.

It seemed the perfect payoff to an introspective morning, during which Saban—arguably history's best college football coach—donned swimming shorts, captained a pontoon boat, and let his hair fly in the wind as he navigated Lake Burton, his second home and refuge, and discussed with Tebow and me the remaining hopes and desires that drive a legendary career. He also spoke of his regrets, his philosophical approach to growing high school boys into NFL men, and his own evolution as a coach and as a man.

I'd never experienced Saban like this. I'm not sure many people have. He was completely disarmed. No football. No veneer. Smoother edges. An easy smile. Jokes. Laughter. He's an elite ballbuster. He enjoyed showing us his jet skis and his boats. He adores this place. The surrounding area is 85 percent national forest; Lake Burton, the first of six lakes in the Tallulah River basin, comprises nearly 2,800 acres and 62 miles of shoreline.

Saban is here three weeks a year. You sense he finds himself during that time.

"I'd like to think that I'm no different than I was when I was a kid growing up in West Virginia, in terms of how I treat people and how important relationships are," he told me, standing alongside the boat bobbing on the water near his dock. "And I think this [lake] gives you a chance to do it. Because I don't think many people here care that you're the coach at Alabama, or how many games you won. And that's refreshing sometimes."

That's not the only way it's refreshing.

Saban loves Lake Burton so much it's his bathtub. During summertime vacation here, he typically plays 18 early holes of golf at the Waterfall Golf Club, of which he is part owner, then heads back to the house to jump into the lake with a bar of Dial soap to scrub up.

You read that right: Nick Saban bathes in Lake Burton.

He loves the water. It seems to buoy him emotionally, to provide some navigation toward perspective. Growing up in West

Virginia, he enjoyed jumping off the waterfalls throughout the mountainous terrain in the area and riding the rapids on his butt.

When he went off to college at Kent State in Ohio, that opportunity did not exist. So when he went home for the summer, the first thing he did was go jump into the river. Lake Burton reminds him of those simpler times.

He used to ski like a madman out here, prior to neck fusion surgery in his early sixties. These days he just cruises. After Saban takes a lake bath, his wife, Ms. Terry, walks down the hill to the dock with a lunch she prepared. On the day we were there, we had chicken salad that tasted like the South, sweet, with a healthy hint of mayonnaise. They take lunch, hop into the pontoon and cruise the lake, and blast the Eagles and the Rolling Stones and Elton John and Michael Jackson so loudly on the speakers that the neighbors joke they're disturbing the peace.

At the time, the country music icon Alan Jackson was Saban's neighbor. Jackson was a valuable resource. When the boat gave Saban trouble, he dialed Jackson for some advice on how he might fix it. Sometimes the Country Music Hall of Famer just walked next door and turned the wrench himself.

"He's [an avid] boat guy and a good mechanic, and he's fixed my boat before," Saban said. "And I sure do appreciate it."

I love country music, so this fascinated me. I wondered if Coach and Alan ever tossed back a couple of beers and fired up the karaoke machine, maybe sang "Between the Devil and Me." Tebow figured their go-to song had to be "Drive." Coach corrected us.

The song he likes is "It's Five O'Clock Somewhere."

We all laughed pretty hard at that.

Coach wanted to drive Tebow and me around the lake in his pontoon boat. We brought some fishing poles. It took about five minutes to realize that was a bad idea. I sat down in the boat and almost instantly felt a stick in my shoulder blade. The fish hook had hung up in my back. So there I was, sitting on Nick Saban's boat, I barely knew him, and he and Tebow were digging a three-pronged barb out of my scapula.

I wasn't embarrassed. But it was an inauspicious moment.

Once I shook the hook we took off. I had a hole in my back, and the fancy new SPF shirt we purchased on the way to the shoot was torn and bloody. But the conversation was free and easy.

"I had great parents," Saban said. "When I was a kid growing up, my dad was sort of a perfectionist. He had high expectations, not just how we played football or baseball, but he had high expectations for how we treated other people, what kind of compassion we had for other people, how we helped other people.

"He'd ask, 'Did you go to church? How did you cut the grass? Did you trim? Did you mow? Did you clean up?' I mean, there was a reckoning for everything that you did."

We all laughed pretty hard at that, too.

He continued: "When you didn't do it right, you had to do it again. When I washed a car and it had streaks in the side, he said, 'Go wash it again.' So I grew up learning that if you didn't do it right, there were going to be consequences that you had to deal with.

"And it was much easier trying to do it the right way the first time."

I felt like I was listening to my dad. For as long as I can remember, my father said, "If you're gonna do it, do it right the first time." Meanwhile, Momma had a cross-stitch hanging on the wall that read, "A stitch in time saves nine." In other words, take your time and do it right so you don't have to correct mistakes.

When we returned to the boathouse, I figured the experience was over. I figured wrong. Saban wanted to jump into the lake like that kid from West Virginia would.

The jump appeared to be about forty feet, down off the platform roof and directly into Lake Burton. Coach Saban drew up the play: He and Tebow would jump simultaneously—Coach aiming right and Tebow aiming left. I'd go last and split them, right down the middle like a game-winning field goal.

And suddenly: *Poof!* They were gone. *Splash.* So there I was, moment of truth, and I began to leap off the roof, and I noticed that Saban didn't go right and Tebow didn't go left, and I'm airborne and they're bobbing right in front of me and I'm thinking: *Oh my God, I'm going to take out Nick Saban* and *Tim Tebow.*

Rather than make national headlines, I contorted my body a bit sideways and missed them. In the process I landed left-ribs-first and damn near knocked the breath out of myself.

We all howled with laughter while trying not to drown. I hollered a *yee haw* like Bo Duke, then dragged myself up onto the dock and doubled over, sucking air.

I thanked Coach for inviting us to his refuge and opening his doors to us.

He reminded me that we had invited ourselves.

And we all laughed pretty damn hard at that, too.

Chapter Two

Just Trust Me

I didn't want to make the phone call. I knew my words would crush my wife but wouldn't shock her. As a reporter's wife, she lived every day braced subconsciously for the unexpected. Sometimes the phone rings and I rush to the airport. That's the job. For several minutes I sat and stared blankly at the wall in my living room, partly euphoric, partly terrified. I fidgeted, sipped my coffee, read and reread the directive.

I dialed her number. As the phone rang in my ear, the emotional roller coaster rose within me, from deep calm to spiking anxiety, that same feeling in your heart and your gut as when the train climbs the rails toward the heavens and the tow chain beckons: *click, click, click.*

She answered the phone with five words: "Where are they sending you?"

Life is about balance and relationships. That applies spiritually and physically. As life progresses and priorities shift, both are increasingly difficult to cultivate and to maintain. We're busy. We get distracted and stressed. We lose touch. Our desires evolve. We seek material things and base importance and self-worth on stuff, not experiences. Bigger house. Nicer car. Fancier clothes.

That's a shame. Because when we're eighty years old and rockin' chairs replace rock 'n' roll, all that stuff means nothing. The experiences and the memories are precious. That's why consciously seeking balance as we feverishly chase dreams is so imperative.

Who we are is so much more important than what we are. That tug-of-war is difficult. The toughest part is the idea that there's always tomorrow; that we'll get to it later. And then later becomes now, and all your kids want from you is money and car keys, not time and attention and affection. And then one day you wake up and your babies are graduating from high school, and you think, *Damn, I should've dressed those dolls with her or thrown him those pitches. Why didn't I? What was so important that I said, "We'll do it later," only to see "later" come and go before we seize the moment?*

It's the story within the seventies Harry Chapin song "Cat's in the Cradle." That song's message is piercing. It scares me because it's true.

I love my job. I love my family.

To excel at both, I have to work for both. Working for both is exhausting. But I don't ever want to look back and wish I'd been more attentive.

I hesitate to explain that battle for me. Though it's not my intention, it will seem exceedingly haughty, because the truth is, my life is a Tiger Woods interview in the morning and a game of H-O-R-S-E with my son in the afternoon—in two different cities after three different airplanes. It's beautifully chaotic. And it requires tremendous selflessness from my wife, Lainie.

Back to that phone call. In retrospect, my response to her intuition was impossibly unfair and self-absorbed.

"If you'll trust me, this will change our lives."

It was November 17, 2014, sometime around seven o'clock on a Monday morning. These are not exact numbers, but at that moment I'd been gone from home for approximately 100 of the past 150 days—or nearly the entire second half of the NASCAR Sprint Cup Series season, spanning a period of time from the final weekend in July to the week before Thanksgiving, and race locations from Indianapolis to Boston to Chicago to Dallas to Phoenix to Miami and little nowhere towns everywhere in between.

Nearly twenty weeks straight, all over the country.

That's hard on a man. It's harder on his spouse.

Children are resilient. They know what they know. And all mine have ever known is that Daddy has to go to the airport. For years they thought my job was flying on airplanes. Sure, they miss Daddy when he's gone, and the older they get the more they say so. But if Mommy is committed to the grind, the kids are committed to the grind without even knowing it.

And to this very moment, Lainie is committed to the grind.

That's not to say she enjoys it.

Lainie and I have three young children. In November 2014 our son, Cambron, celebrated his ninth birthday. Our daughters, Mia and Vivian, were five and two, respectively. Those are wonderfully tough ages.

And it deserves noting that Lainie and I don't have a standard parenting scenario, if there is such a thing. Cambron has Tourette's syndrome, and as most Tourette's parents will attest, a myriad of complicated variables accompany that. Tics. Outbursts. Attention deficit issues. Social anxiety. Raising any child is challenging. Raising a child with a neurological condition presents additional difficulties. Many parents today can relate.

But don't get it twisted. We have no complaints. Our blessings overflow. We're exceedingly proud of Cambron. God blessed us richly with his perspective, no matter how confusing and frustrating that perspective can sometimes be to those of us who don't share it. He's a special person who constantly teaches me more about myself than anyone else can. I adore my son. I am so proud of him. I love you, buddy.

On November 17, 2014, I was the lead reporter for ESPN's NASCAR coverage, and at the time the network was in the last season of an eight-year agreement to nationally broadcast the final twenty races of the sport's premier series.

I wasn't part of the actual racing broadcast team. Instead, I reported news, conducted interviews, and produced feature pieces that aired on the network's ancillary programming, shows like *SportsCenter* and the *NASCAR Countdown* prerace program.

That meant I lived on airplanes and in hotel rooms. And that meant Lainie was alone, a lot, managing our children and our home. The mom routine is monotonous and unrelenting: Alarm. Snooze. Alarm. Wake up. Peel self from bed. Stumble to kids' rooms. Wake kids. Strip urine-drenched sheets. Laundry. Juices. Medicines. Breakfasts. Pack lunches. Pack backpacks. Dress Mia. Dress Vivian. Hope Cambron got dressed. Hope Cambron brushed his teeth. Buckle up. Traffic. Car pool. Traffic. Drop-off. Traffic. Laundry. Grocery store. Traffic. Car pool. Traffic. Practice. Traffic. Dinner. Dishes. Pajamas. Bedtime story. Prayers. Pound wine. Fall into couch.

If you don't respect a stay-at-home mother, you're just ignorant.

By the time she got ten minutes alone, she'd spent nine hours in the car. Lainie was a different brand of exhausted.

I've always respected and honored that effort, with consideration that so much of what she manages is intangible. There's no office or title. There's just work and love.

I strive to supplement that effort when I'm at home. Supplement, not overtake. One thing I've learned over the past decade about being a traveling parent: It's important to inject harmony into the home upon arrival, not rewrite the daily itinerary or parental philosophy based on my own rigid approach or selfish desires.

I tried that too often in our earlier stages of parenthood. If there was disharmony when I got home from the road, I'd instantly jump in to strong-arm it into accord. It's a futile approach. I hadn't been there. I didn't know context. So who was I to inject any opinion? Again, Lainie is astute. Her patient approach taught me this.

On the morning of November 17, 2014, my lone focus when I walked in the front door of our suburban Charlotte home—the kind with dual-floor, white front porches—and past my cluttered office, which had long been the bane of Lainie's existence, and beyond the beige microfiber couch commanding our living room, was to be present for my family.

Dad. Husband. Friend.

I don't remember much about the moment when that all changed. I was in a mental fog from a late night at the racetrack and a predawn flight from Miami to Charlotte. I aimed my path toward the island in my kitchen, dodging our kids' toys. Our wood floors are perpetually littered with countless pink and blue Barbie accessories and Minecraft figurines and superballs and stuffed animals.

It looked like the county fair had exploded in there.

I rounded the corner to my right to see Lainie standing on the far side of the island, leaned up against our dishwasher. She was preparing the kids' morning routine: juices, vitamins, and breakfasts.

She didn't look at me. Didn't run and jump into my arms. It stripped me, that moment. Whoever said absence makes the heart grow fonder never traveled for a living. They went on vacation for a week or something.

Lainie had tears in her eyes. She'd been a single mother for five months.

"I need you home, Martin."

Those words were completely understandable. But they hurt. And for me as a traveling father, at that time, they targeted a distinct insecurity.

"I know. I'm here now."

"No. I mean I need you here, for like a month."

Lainie was cooked. She needed and deserved a break. She needed her partner. She needed her husband and the father of her children to be present and engaged. She needed to feel love and appreciation and awareness and respect.

"Don't worry. ESPN won't call me until January 1, if then. I'm here for almost two months."

My third Disney contract was set to commence on New Year's Day, 2015. At that moment, I was uncertain what my job would even entail. For sixteen years—from the moment I graduated college— all I'd covered professionally, full-time, was auto racing. It was all I knew.

But beginning in 2015, ESPN would no longer broadcast NAS-CAR. Earlier that year NBC had bought the rights package for the next decade, which meant ESPN was out until at least 2024.

After nearly two decades in the garage, the idea of professional diversity interested me. So I made the decision to remain at ESPN and see where the ride led.

And what a ride. The moments experienced and relationships built and interviews conducted have been beyond my most fantastic childhood dreams.

They are genuinely unfathomable. And they are the reason this book exists.

That November morning is why those experiences exist.

Lainie and I embraced and she departed to load Cambron and

Mia into the car for the daily commute to school. I poured a cup of coffee, added cinnamon, milk, and honey, and eased into the couch with the cleansing exhale of a lengthy task completed.

I turned on the television, removed my phone from my pocket, and opened my email.

That's the moment everything changed.

Atop the page was a note sent from ESPN executive Lee Fitting, the mind behind the *College GameDay* phenomenon. Lee assumed leadership of a good preview show and made it an institution—when he took it on the road to the people. He enlisted A-list celebrities to pick winners of the week's most impactful games. He highlighted wacky handmade posters spotted in the live campus crowd. He propelled his on-air personalities into household names, and in the process developed a three-hour must-watch staple, as synonymous with the culture and tradition and passion of college football as the games themselves. The *GameDay* influence only grows larger in prestige and impact every year.

Fitting's email was a road map to my future. It was like the message in a bottle that washes onto the beach and leads directly to the buried treasure: If you're willing to dig deep, life-changing riches await. Fitting stated that he enjoyed my passionate approach to reporting, and that he and other ESPN executives believed my style belonged in college football.

The email instructed me to start studying hard, because in one month I would be one of the four reporters he would embed within one of the four programs in the inaugural College Football Playoff games.

I could neither believe nor comprehend what I was reading.

Holy smokes.

I read the email again. I stifled my glee. I called Lainie.

She knew.

"Where are they sending you?" she answered.

She honest to God answered the phone with that statement.

"The inaugural College Football Playoff. It's one of the most important initiatives and partnerships in the company. It's a monster stage. *And, oh my God, it's college f——football.*"

Those words didn't register with Lainie. She doesn't care about sports, so at that moment I was speaking a foreign language. Attempting to explain to her the magnitude of the College Football Playoff games was like explaining the Pythagorean theorem: Okay, fine, it *sounds* important. But who gives a damn and why do I care?

Then I said it: "If you'll trust me, this will change our lives."

It was a ridiculous, unfair, self-righteous statement.

I didn't even know if it was true.

But I believed it was true.

Lainie will tell you she had no say in the matter. She's right. I saw our future in that email. I saw the potential in that treasure map. I saw it leading to a life-changing destination.

She saw another month of single motherhood.

Sports just isn't her thing. That's not to say she doesn't support every opportunity I'm given, because she absolutely and wholeheartedly does, without complaint and with bursting pride. But she doesn't discuss the job unless someone else broaches the subject with her.

Truth is, she'd rather meet Jordan Rodgers than Michael Jordan.

Ironically, that's a wonderful brand of spousal support. She doesn't kiss my ass. Ever. We won't take our identity from the job, even though that's sometimes difficult for me, and something I, like most men, personally battle. She tells me the truth—even when it's difficult to hear.

Though I'm plenty flawed and have made hurtful mistakes, she's proud of me as a man—far more than as a broadcaster or as a writer. She's prouder that I've taken a red-eye home for preschool graduation to sit alongside her and snap a thousand obnoxious pictures of our children than she is that I have interviewed Rory McIlroy or Urban Meyer. That's just the truth.

Speaking of Meyer, he plays a considerable role in this story.

When I hung up the phone with Lainie, I replied to Fitting.

All in. Let's go. Thank you so much for believing.

It was an anomaly. Unprecedented might be inaccurate and melodramatic. But if it's not unprecedented, it's close. Sportscentric reporters don't just up and change sports—especially after seventeen years. It just doesn't happen.

Imagine ESPN NFL insider Adam Schefter, synonymous with the National Football League, reporting from a baseball clubhouse about Bryce Harper. Or even more applicable, Barry Melrose— who *is* the National Hockey League on ESPN—standing on the first fairway at the Augusta National Golf Club, reporting on golf. It would be weird, right?

Neither of those scenarios would be nearly as shocking to sports fans as mine was during that first College Football Playoff. One reason is my accent. It's Southern and it's thick and it's proud, and understandably at the time, everyone associated it immediately with NASCAR. So when I landed in Columbus, Ohio, with Meyer and the Buckeyes, ESPN viewers wondered what in the *hell* was going on.

They weren't alone.

The day I arrived at Ohio State, I made what proved to be a shrewd decision: Report what you see and what you think is interesting. Do not attempt to dive too deeply into the intricacies of the players or the team dynamic. If you get too cute and try to look too smart and aren't authentic, and don't speak the verbiage quite right, you'll look foolish and be exposed immediately.

College football fans—especially the blue bloods—take their identities from the teams they love. It's an all-day, everyday, life-long love affair. They know every detail and nuance. And they know when you don't. And when you don't, and try to act as though you do, those fans take it personally.

I walked in the door a couple of days after Christmas. We were stationed in a corner at the far end of a hundred-yard hall-way within the Woody Hayes Athletic Center, where the OSU Buckeyes football headquarters is located. Our position was at the hallway elbow between the graduate assistants and the video staff. Tucked within our little nook, over to the right, was a green board covered in the white chalk strokes of Coach Hayes's handwriting.

When he died in 1987, Coach Hayes had been devising a book on leadership. The writing on that chalkboard is a fascinating peek into his philosophical approach, divided into topical chapters that suggested Coach Hayes hadn't quite corralled his thoughts just yet. The chapters are numbered and titled with words like "Other Side Of Coin," "Around The Table (incl. heroes)," "Bor-rowers," "Things Better Not Said (Press?)," and "Fixed Lines and Fixed Opinions." The Ohio State staff found the chalkboard in a dusty back closet decades after Hayes passed away, encased it in glass, and hung it on the wall to memorialize the beloved Buck-eyes coach. On the wall above it, in silver lettering, read the words: Woody's Final Thoughts: Football—The Military—His Country.

The Ohio State sports information director, Jerry Emig, greeted me with a large smile. He's a very kind man, and he was immensely helpful to me throughout that assignment. I peppered him with ele-mentary questions for a month—sometimes repetitively to ensure accuracy—and he answered them with great patience and precision.

Eventually, on the third day or so, he strolled over and told me I should meet Coach Meyer. Down the hallway and into Meyer's office we went. He's an intense man, especially when the National

Championship is within his grasp and the entire nation gives him no chance to win it.

I shook his hand, looked him in the eye, and told him what a pleasure it was to meet him. That was the extent of the conversation. He wasn't cold. But he wasn't warm, either.

Behind memorable performances by future NFL Pro Bowlers Ezekiel Elliott, Michael Thomas, and Joey Bosa, and movie-script third-string quarterback Cardale Jones, Ohio State went on to upset Alabama in the Sugar Bowl, and to then dominate Oregon in the National Championship game. They won the whole damn thing.

And I was there for the entire ride. Even writing that sentence makes me shake my head in disbelief that it's true.

There was a specific moment during the Buckeyes' championship run that validated my day-one philosophy. It happened in the final moments of Sugar Bowl media day, somewhere near the 10-yard line on the playing surface at the New Orleans Superdome.

During media day, players and coaches are made available to the assembled members of the press corps. They sit at individual tables or stages positioned on the field and answer questions for about an hour.

Earlier that week I had asked Emig to secure me a sleeve of Buckeye helmet stickers, the white circular ones adorned by the green sprig, the ones highlighted in the ESPN television commercials. BUCKEYE!

I always found those stickers to be interesting and iconic, and I wondered what they meant to the players.

I wandered around the Superdome to find out. I asked Elliott. I asked Bosa. I asked Thomas. I asked Jones. I asked Eli Apple. I asked Curtis Samuel. I asked Joshua Perry. On and on, these young star players all had similar answers. If they completed this play or that task during a game, they earned a sticker.

No. That's not what I wanted. I didn't care about how the stickers were earned.

I cared about what they meant.

On the brink of giving up, I approached one last player with the sleeve of stickers and the request for their importance—wide receiver Devin Smith, jersey number 9, the team's deep threat on the perimeter.

He answered something about special teams. Frustrated, I tried again: "No, dammit. Devin, what does this f—— sticker *mean* to you, man?"

His answer was like the skies parting: "Oh. Okay. I see what you mean, Mr. Marty. Yes I do. That sticker is Cris Carter calling me at seven o'clock in the morning on game day, to make sure I'm prepared to uphold the tradition of *the* Ohio State University. That sticker is Archie Griffin, waiting on me as I enter the locker room on game day, to make sure that I'm prepared to uphold the tradition of *the* Ohio State University. That sticker is Eddie George, waiting on me in the tunnel before I run on the field, to make sure I'm prepared to uphold the tradition of *the* Ohio State University. That sticker is Orlando Pace…"

You get the idea. Devin named five or six all-world Ohio State football legends. I got chills. Devin just smiled.

I saved that little nugget of information until the evening of the Sugar Bowl. Buckeye fans still approach me about it in airports and restaurants.

Fast-forward one year.

The 2015 College Football Playoff National Championship was held at the University of Phoenix Stadium, out in the desert. The Toaster. It was the first of four consecutive playoff installments between Clemson and Alabama. Saban versus Dabo Swinney. Deshaun Watson against the Tide.

As part of ESPN's championship coverage, the network invited a trio of elite coaches to serve as *GameDay* guest analysts: Brian Kelly from Notre Dame, Hugh Freeze from Ole Miss—and Urban Meyer. It was interesting to watch them interact. They didn't speak much. After one midday live shot, Meyer asked to chat with me. I walked over to the couch and took a knee beside the arm of the couch on which he sat.

"I need to tell you something," he said.

"Yessir."

"Remember when we met? You were on campus with us last year, and walked into my office?"

"Yessir. I recall it very well."

"I have to tell you, when you walked in, I thought, 'Wait a minute, now—Florida State gets Tom Rinaldi, Oregon gets Samantha Ponder, Alabama gets Kaylee Hartung...

"'And we get this redneck from NASCAR? That's what they think of us?'"

I wasn't sure what to make of that statement.

And then he grinned. And then we both laughed.

He had a point. Rinaldi is the standard by which all other sports reporters are measured. During the inaugural playoff, he was embedded with the Florida State Seminoles. Ponder was the most popular reporter at the entire network. She was with the Oregon Ducks. Hartung was the sweetheart of the SEC. She was with Bama.

And the Buckeyes got the bumpkin.

Then Meyer told me something that will always stick with me: It took him one week to realize that I was different. The passion fit the program. I was the right guy at the right time with the right team.

Like the Buckeyes, I was the underdog nobody believed should be there.

Nobody except the people in their own house, anyway.

I am so grateful that Lainie believed in me and sacrificed for me. Because it absolutely changed our lives.

Chapter Three

We're Not Gonna Do That

When college football fans give me grief for spending extensive time in towns other than their own—and they do, often—I have a standard explanation: I go where they're good.

They're damn good in Clemson, South Carolina, home of the Tigers and steeped in tradition; and since 2015 I've spent as much time in Clemson as anywhere on earth. I joke that I need an apartment there. (I really do need an apartment there.)

After the Tigers won the 2016 National Championship, President Donald Trump invited Clemson head coach Dabo Swinney and the boys to the White House, to celebrate and to be acknowledged for the accomplishment, as many championship teams customarily do. ESPN, in turn, sent my team and me to Washington, DC, to cover the landmark day.

It was a landmark day for us, too. For very different reasons.

It was a Monday. And it was hot enough to make the devil sigh. Before Clemson arrived, I was on-site at the White House previewing the Tigers' visit on various ESPN programs. One of those programs was the *Dan Le Batard Show*, an irreverent ESPN radio extravaganza. The show is simulcast on television, live, from the Clevelander Hotel in South Beach, and features hosts Dan Le Batard and Jon Weiner, whom the world knows as Stugotz, which Dan tells me is an Italian word that translates into English as "bull testicles" or something.

I adore both men, the main reason being that their give-a-damns are broke. They never take themselves too seriously. That reminds listeners that it's okay to laugh and it's important to wonder aloud about things that inspire wonder. Their show inspires me to think and to be unafraid to create and be weird. Most of us are weird. Own your weird.

Publicly they have very distinct personalities: Dan is a classic skeptic, unafraid to ask any question of anyone. Stu plays the village idiot, who is in fact smarter than you are. Together they are brilliant. Together they beat the system; they built a sports radio empire by mocking traditional sports radio. ESPN is very fortunate to have them. They are the antithesis of the standard ESPN model.

Away from the mayhem, both are caring people who open their hearts to friends. I once saw Dan in a telling moment of compassion toward his father. I was a guest host on Dan's daily television program, *Highly Questionable*, which features his father, Papi, as a cohost. (That's the dream—get paid to hang out with your ol' man and talk ball.)

We were sitting at the desk on-set, taping the program, and Papi was to read some jokes off a teleprompter. He got a bit frustrated trying to read one particular line. He tried several times and grew more flustered each time.

Dan took him by the hand and said sweetly, "Papi. It's okay. Take as much time as you need. We're not in a hurry. You'll get it."

It was quite a moment. Don't go thinking it was cheesy or some sort of put-on, either. It was genuinely sweet. (And Dan might junk-punch me for telling it, because that moment was the polar opposite of his brand.) I'd never seen Dan in loving-son mode. My respect for him professionally was already lofty. Just then that respect transitioned from professional to personal.

I miss my daddy terribly, so to see a man appreciate and respect and care for his own father moved me.

On the *Dan Le Batard Show* set, a glass partition separates the studio from the control room, in which a group of young producers named Billy and Roy and Chris and Mike hang out. They all play pivotal roles. Other than Mike, I'm not sure what the hell any of them do. But their collective sense of humor is infectious. Another producer, Allyson, is the show's conductor, charged with keeping this South Beach yard sale on the rails.

As a team, the *Le Batard Show* boys are magic. Their following is a massive, loyal cult. And being a member of their recurring cast of diverse characters is indescribably beneficial to all whom they champion. That includes me.

On the day we were in Washington with Clemson, I was scheduled to appear on their program in the late morning, live, from a location just off the White House lawn that political reporters call Pebble Beach. It's the position you see reporters in every night on all the news programs, with the White House behind them in the background, stark and stately, pointed toward Pennsylvania Avenue.

During the live shot, which could be seen on television and heard on the radio, my love of throwing footballs was broached. I am Uncle Rico from the movie *Napoleon Dynamite*. Throwing footballs is a joy I'll never outgrow. I've thrown more passes on television than some NFL backup quarterbacks.

Spontaneously, during the interview, I sent my audio technician Cory Harrilchak out for a post pattern.

He ran toward a tree.

On the North Lawn of the White House.

I threw him a pass, maybe 25 or 30 yards in length. He caught it. Nothing spectacular, other than the fact that he ran a post pattern in Trump's yard.

The Le Batard boys fell out. Just lost it. They were roaring with laughter.

And they wanted us to do it again.

But before we could do it again, a gentleman, a reporter maybe, I wish I knew his name, leaped from his post near ours on Pebble Beach, peeked around the green awning partition between our sections, and said, stone-faced, "If you do that again, you'll get shot."

We hadn't considered the fact that the Secret Service boys' gun sights were likely trained on Cory's forehead.

So I turned back to the camera, a few shades of respect paler now, and told Dan and Stu: "They said if we do that again, we'll get shot. So we're not gonna do that."

We're not certain, but we'd like to believe we're the only QB/wide receiver tandem to complete an unscripted pass on the White House lawn.

We are also very thankful that the Secret Service has a sense of humor.

Exile

On the Marty Smith's America podcast, ESPN host Dan Le Batard shared with me his perspective on his parents' exile from Cuba to the United States; they were in search of one thing: freedom. He details how he and his brother, Lebo, are the beneficiaries of that sacrifice—and why the Le Batard family story is a Miami story.

They left Cuba in their teens, thrown to the wind, almost literally, by the grandparents who worried about the regime that was coming. Imagine that. The ocean is filled between Miami and Cuba with those stories and those bodies, literally. I'm not saying that metaphorically. The ocean is filled with people that have thrown their lives or their children's lives to the wind to get to freedom. My parents are not immigrants. They are exiles. They had money in Cuba. They were happy in Cuba. Their families were happy in Cuba. They left money for poverty because of how much they value freedom. They built a life here, through a great many struggles, with my father working as a waiter; my father, without speaking English, got a master's degree in engineering and they made a life for themselves. It was a hard life; it was rough. And I never experienced any of that because they protected me and my brother from all of it so we could create. So we could just be creators. My brother is a professional artist, very successful, and these are not easy professions. Writing and art are not easy professions. But it all starts there, because they made exile sacrifices. That, in many ways, is the story of Miami. Miami is built on those kind of stories—parents who made sacrifices so the kids could have freedom.

Chapter Four

Olivia

I want to tell you about a friend of mine. Political correctness says I'm not supposed to call her special. But that's what she is to me. She's special.

Her name was Olivia Quigley. She was beautiful without trying, a runner and a fighter, and by way of both, a leader by example, graceful and compassionate and doggedly determined, simply profound, a burst of light through a maze of emotional darkness that traps many like her—darkness born from ignorance and insecurity within the rest of us—from which, for some for far too long, an exit seems futile.

Olivia had autism. It was a condition. Not a definition.

Our relationship was brief. But its impact was global and powerful and eternal.

We all have moments in our daily lives that present split-second decisions that may or may not be life altering. Like the hitchhiker thumbing for a ride on a frigid afternoon, or the homeless person stationed at the stoplight near the interstate off-ramp, holding a tattered scrap of cardboard, pleading via strokes of black marker for food or shelter or work.

What to do? The internal debate immediately swirls: Do we extend a sympathetic hand and share a blessing? Or do we cruise on by and leave the same decision to the next passerby?

When I choose the latter (which admittedly is too often), I wonder if I should have extended that hand—and more importantly, why I didn't. Invariably a sense of emptiness emerges, overwhelming empathy mixed with guilt. For me, for some reason, the emotion is acute but fleeting, gone as quickly as it arrived.

And for as long as I can remember, seeing someone seated alone—especially while dining in public—has made me sad. I have no idea why. It shouldn't. Lainie constantly reminds me how much some actually *enjoy* solitude.

I never want to be alone.

And I never want to wonder, *What if?*

That's why I approached Olivia. It was late July 2015 when I walked into a bustling track stadium at the University of California, Riverside. Not quite noon but already sweltering, the opening practice for the Special Olympics World Summer Games was sprinting into its third hour.

Athletes from across the United States were there, running and jumping past prejudice and predisposition. The scene was a statement, a portrait of defiant achievement. These were activities doctors and therapists had long said many of them would never enjoy.

Special Olympics athletes are accustomed to overcoming ignorance and intolerance and downright nastiness. They are accustomed to hearing "You can't…" and "You won't…" and "You'll never…" Many of them are mocked and ridiculed for the uniqueness their respective intellectual disabilities produce. World Games are their opportunity to flip the bird at the notion that they're incapable or different or somehow less.

Not all of them know that. But some certainly do. Olivia most certainly did.

World Games athletes are all achievers. They're all welcome. They're all equal and important. They're *included*. The pride that accompanies inclusion is palpable. Being a part of something is empowering.

Joy hung in the air that day, that carefree purity that envelops you when children laugh.

Standing on the orange rubber running surface, United States track-and-field coach Bonnie Kahn detailed the impact and intricacies of the World Games, and offered some information about her athletes that I might use during ESPN's live, three-hour broadcast of the Opening Ceremony two days later.

That brings us to Olivia. As Coach Kahn spoke, I looked to my left. There, seated alone on an aluminum bench—the kind you'd see on the sidelines at a high school football game—sat a young lady, staring blankly toward the ground, stretching her legs.

Honestly, I didn't yet know it was a young lady.

The person was bald.

Intrigued, I excused myself and walked over to the bench to sit down. I asked what she was doing over here all by herself.

"I'm just so tired," she said.

"Tired? The Games have only just begun. Why are you tired?"

"Chemotherapy."

Time stopped.

Olivia was twenty-four years old, a sprinter from Wisconsin. It was fitting that she was a sprinter. Her entire life, she outran fear and pain and doubt. In doing so, she taught others how to outrun them, too. Funny thing was, she never ran *from* anything.

On that hot July day, her mental push was intact, as focused and courageous as ever. She was elegant in speech and confident in cadence. Olivia explained autism to me from her perspective. When she spoke, her eyes chased mine, as if to make certain I processed the words she said.

Months earlier, in February 2015, Olivia had been diagnosed with stage 4 breast cancer. Chemotherapy sapped her stamina. It did not touch her spirit. Her mother, Judy, later told me Olivia's incredibly kind heart and compassion provided the fuel that kept her going. She noted Olivia's indomitable determination. She simply refused to quit. Ever.

Judy and her husband, Dan, adopted Olivia from China in 1994, when Olivia was three years old. They did not know she had an intellectual disability until months after they returned home, to Elm Grove, Wisconsin. For years, doctors cautioned the Quigleys to not set high expectations for Olivia. They said she'd never hold a job or live alone.

Those doctors were wrong.

Judy and Dan wouldn't accept pessimism. They enrolled Olivia in a program called Project SEARCH, a workplace immersion program that combines classroom instruction, career exploration, and hands-on training through worksite rotations.

Olivia received hands-on work experience, and she eventually earned a full-time job at Children's Hospital of Wisconsin as a room service attendant. She was also active in sports, reaching the high-brown belt level in tae kwon do by training multiple days per week.

And she began running, which was a gift that would ultimately become a platform.

When she was invited to the World Games, Olivia informed her oncologist that she would halt chemotherapy until the competition was complete. Nothing would deter her goal: to medal. As she told me, a medal would provide an example to women all over the world of what they could achieve while battling the faceless, ruthless foe of cancer.

It had all started with tremendous pain. That was notable, Olivia told me, because she had a lofty pain tolerance. Her breasts were swollen and bruised. She didn't discuss it with Judy; she didn't want to bother her mother with it. Finally, though, she couldn't tolerate it any longer.

She called Judy on the phone and described the pain: It felt like everything inside her was on fire, burning up. An ultrasound was performed, revealing massive, cancerous tumors in Olivia's breasts—so large that doctors prescribed six months of chemo treatments to shrink them.

Chemotherapy made Olivia very sick. But chemo also saved her life.

The dichotomy troubled her as much as it inspired her.

She told me then, "If I didn't have chemotherapy, I wouldn't be standing here today."

As she said this, practice concluded and the team gathered around Coach Kahn for an inspirational message and some instruction. Olivia approached me once more.

"Will you please tell everyone how positive I am?" she asked. "I'm a really positive person. I want people to know that."

I was taken with her fundamental approach to happiness. Be positive. Be kind. Laugh hard. Try hard. Focus your effort on those who reciprocate. Smile. Her intentions were always genuine. Her perspective was always just and sweet. Olivia knew no judgment of others. She was not superficial. We did not make small talk or feel each other out or search for reasons why the conversation mattered.

It just mattered.

We all can learn a lot from that.

It became my mission to tell her story. She would go on to win gold medals in the 100-meter sprint and the 400-meter relay, surging victorious to the finish before falling flat from sheer exhaustion at the finish line. Her courage made her the face of the 2015 Special Olympics World Summer Games. Olivia was named one of the twenty-five most influential women in sports by ESPN's female-focused website, ESPNW, and she was honored in New York City for her courage and kindness and example.

And she became my friend. I cried when she won the 100. Many of us did. Judy and Dan are remarkably strong, composed people, realists, doers not followers. They cried, too. That gold medal was the culmination of years spent searching for affirmation and belonging.

After the World Games, Olivia and I stayed in touch, exchanging text messages and speaking on the phone. Each time I was reminded of the time Judy had shared a concept with me about her daughter: There is beauty in simplicity, so accurate and so powerful. Olivia's perspective was so simple, and therefore, in this fractured world, so profound.

Olivia is the consummate example of the Special Olympics' power and impact. Judy once told me there were times in Olivia's life when Olivia was very frustrated and angry, and that her experience at the World Games helped change that. It infused her with self-confidence. Olivia's confidence, Judy told me, enabled the Quigley family to interact as adults for the first time.

Think about that. That's the power of sports. And compassion. Confidence. Belonging. Support. That medal helped improve an entire familial dynamic.

Grace is omnipresent but demands awareness. Maybe it's a smile from a stranger that improves your mood. Maybe it's a guy letting you into traffic that offers the precious moments needed to arrive on time. Maybe it's help changing a tire or watching the kids while you run out to complete an errand or forgiveness received for a stupid mistake. Maybe it's a simple hello.

All of that is grace. And that was Olivia, all the time. She put others first in her thoughts and hopes, as we all should strive to do.

In the summer of 2016, Olivia won another gold medal in the

100 meters, this time at the Wisconsin Special Olympics Summer Games. At that same time she began experiencing severe headaches, and a cancerous tumor was discovered in her brain. Despite surgery to remove the tumor, the cancer continued to spread.

In March 2017, after a two-year battle with cancer, Olivia died. She was twenty-five years old. She taught me so much during our friendship, and she continues to teach me even after her passing.

There is a thin black box in the top drawer of the desk in my home office. It is velvet, four inches by four inches square. On one side there is a pair of brass hinges, which are broken, separating the top of the box from the bottom. In the middle, inch-thick gray foam padding surrounds a circular cutout, an indentation.

Every now and then I open the drawer to find the box, mainly when I pause to consider the greater plan for my life and what I believe to be my purpose. Because the box's contents represent my bigger-picture aspiration:

Kindness and joy.

Accompanying the box is a letter, written on white stationery with a shimmery gold border. It is from Judy, and she explains that before her death, Olivia created a brief last will and testament.

Within that will, there were instructions to send her 100-meter gold medal to "a very kind guy," her "special friend."

She willed her 100-meter gold medal to me.

I weep every time I think about her considering that.

It makes me feel very small.

I will carry her achievement, her example—and her precious soul—with me for all my days.

Chapter Five

Define Your Own Life

Tim Tebow had never seen me fragile before. I'm a pretty intense person, and I'm almost always happy. So when I'm lethargic or reserved, it is easily noticed. We had just helicoptered off the flight deck of the USS *Carl Vinson* Navy aircraft carrier, where we had spent the past couple of days living with the sailors and learning about their vital occupations aboard the ship.

We landed at the San Diego Airport, exited the chopper, and boarded Tim's plane for a flight to San Antonio. While we were seated diagonally across from each other, I began to discuss some of my insecurities. His facial expression changed. His eyes narrowed and he sat up and pointed at my face.

"Define your own life. Do not let anyone else define your life. No one else gets that right. Do not let anyone take that right from you. Because they don't have that right."

Timmy was right, certainly. But setting a definition and living a definition aren't always one and the same.

I like to be liked. And I hate it.

It is a character flaw of mine. I wish I didn't care what you think of me. I've whittled life off my years caring what others think. I wish I were self-confident enough to walk through my hours and days carefree and unimpeded, with no consideration of outside opinion—good or bad—regarding who and what I am. But I don't let on; rather, I just consume the criticism, listen, adhere, and move on, most times stewing over my true feelings on the matter for hours afterward.

Sometimes this exercise will emotionally derail my entire day.

It is exhausting. And I'm not alone. Many of you are nodding your heads in agreement right now. This is a relatable concern, especially in today's world in which criticism and hatred come from so many faceless directions. Folks who live freely don't care how they're perceived or yearn for affirmation. They just live, confidently.

Tebow inspires me that way. Just do you, man. Tim does Tim, all day, every day. It's inspiring.

Every time I'm with Tebow I'm inspired. I've never met anyone quite like him. He seems completely unaffected by anything but the path he's on, which he believes is preordained. He lives fearlessly, above the fray, devoid of the emotional extremes that accompany outside opinion. Most of us are obsessed with how others perceive us, and our decisions and our directions are heavily influenced by the desire to meet, exceed, or debunk those perceptions.

That shouldn't be the case. But we can't help it.

Not Tim. He'll tell you his belief is indomitable because his faith is unwavering. He's spent more than a decade disproving nonbelievers—and I don't mean non-Christians. I mean all those guys who said he couldn't play quarterback in the NFL and all those guys who mocked him when he told the world he was chasing baseball. The difference with Tim was, he genuinely didn't listen. Most of us pretend not to listen, but we do.

Tim is a better man than I am. His compass doesn't bounce around the dial, trying to find direction at every turn. It's always pointed forward.

"I want to be someone that pursues whatever is on my heart with everything that I have," Tebow told me as we stood in his kitchen on a sunny Monday in Jacksonville, Florida. "And if I fall flat on my face, then guess what, Marty? I'm going to get right back up. I'm going to do it giving everything that I have, every single time."

That's what led me to his house. That philosophy right there. Why was this Heisman Trophy–winning quarterback, who hadn't played baseball in a decade, trying to play professionally? Why not just ease into the television analyst role he could hold for the next forty years? Didn't he realize that pro ballplayers spend lifetimes honing every minute detail of the game, studying its infinite nuances, slogging through the minor leagues for years for just a prayer of going to the Show? Some guys played three years in college, while some took a chance directly from high school. Most of them never sniffed a single inning in the Show. And here this quarterback came, waltzing in from the gridiron and the television set, thinking he'd show up and ball?

Didn't he realize how ridiculous and futile that seemed? Didn't he hear the incessant noise that it must be a publicity stunt, that the New York Mets' decision to sign him was a joke?

No. He did not. Because for him, it was neither ridiculous nor futile. And it certainly was no publicity stunt. Publicity stunts don't ride the team bus from one nowhere town to the next in the middle of the night for months on end.

He was not playing baseball for anyone else. He was playing baseball for himself. Because he could.

"I hope what me playing baseball says, is that there's certain things in life that we love, and that we have chances to pursue, but a lot of the time the fear of the unknown, the fear of failure, gets in the way," Tebow said. "And I don't want that fear to stop me from trying to be what I want to be, as an athlete, as a person, as a Christian, the way I treat people; I don't want that fear to creep in."

That fear limits most of us. We won't try because we don't want to fail. Failure breeds insecurity, dents our confidence. And when you're in the public eye the way Tebow is, failure creates a basketball-sized bull's-eye, the easiest of targets. When he announced he would pursue baseball, the criticism was merciless. Some called him a farce. Some a joke. Some an embarrassment, not just to himself but to the game of baseball. I've met few individuals so graceful in response to criticism.

"I'm so thankful that I don't have to read it, I don't have to listen to it, I don't have to live the roller coaster that the rest of the world lives of my life," Tebow said. "I don't have to go through the highs and lows. I don't have to be defined by what a writer thinks. I don't have to be defined by what a journalist thinks.

"I'm defined by a couple of things: First and foremost, my relationship with Jesus Christ. Then, how do I treat my family? And then, what am I doing for the rest of the world? And because of that, I can go pursue what is on my heart with everything that I have, with full conviction, with full passion for it, leaving nothing, going after it with everything I have with reckless abandon because, at the end of the day, I don't have to report to a journalist.

"I don't care what they write about me. They've written a lot of things over the last fifteen years about me, some good, some not good, some just 'cause they want to sell papers. I don't necessarily care. I want to pursue my passion, because I believe when you're pursuing what's on your heart, when you're pursuing what you're convicted by, then [you] don't have to live with regret ten, fifteen, twenty years from now, looking back [and] saying, 'What if? What if I would've tried that? What if I would've done that? Would I live with less regret now?' I want to be someone who truly lives life with reckless abandon, so I don't have to look back twenty years from now and say, 'What if?'"

This was the opportunity to chase one boyhood dream after

he'd already lived another. Wouldn't we all take that chance? I'd like to believe I would.

"When I was four, five, six years old, baseball was my first love," Tebow said. "Most of my life I thought I was going to pursue baseball as a profession. I thought about going pro out of high school. Dad was actually kind of pushing me that way, but Mom wanted me to get an education—and this guy named Urban Meyer had something to say about that, too.

"So I decided to go to Florida. It was the second-hardest decision in my life, choosing what I was going to do. I was either going to stay and play my senior year of baseball in high school, and try to go pro out of high school, or I was going to go to the University of Florida early and go pursue football. I remember sitting on the edge of my bed, crying over it."

He chose football. It worked out all right. Tim led the Gators to the 2006 and 2008 Southeastern Conference and National Championships, and in 2007 he earned one of the most prestigious individual awards in sports, the Heisman Trophy, given to the best player in college football. The Denver Broncos selected Tebow in the twenty-fifth overall pick of the 2010 NFL Draft. Late that season he won the starting job, and in his second season he led the Broncos to a playoff victory over the Pittsburgh Steelers.

That game, though, was effectively the end of Tebow's football career. The Broncos traded him away to the New York Jets, and he bounced around from there to the New England Patriots and the Philadelphia Eagles, but he never saw appreciable playing time again.

"I don't regret *a thing*," Tebow told me.

Standing in his Jacksonville home, across the kitchen island from me, Tebow cut an impressive form: six foot three, 255 pounds of muscle, perfect hair, easy smile, comfortable posture. He looked more like a football player than ever. I had wondered for years why he didn't pursue another position on the football field. Pride? With that size and athleticism—he ran a 6.6-second 60-yard dash during a baseball showcase prior to signing with the Mets—certainly he could play tight end.

At the time, he told me that as many as five teams called his agent every single day with inquiries about whether he might consider playing tight end, running back, or H-back, a perimeter skill position that would accentuate his athleticism with the ball in his hands. He had no interest whatsoever. That made no sense to me.

"Would that be exciting? Would that be fun? Absolutely," he said. "I love the game of football, but that's not my passion. It's never where my heart was. The biggest reason I love the game of football is because, when we were down six [points] with two minutes to go, and I was standing in that huddle, the other team guys would look at me and they would be depending on me to get the job done. That's what I loved the most about football.

"If now that's not what I get to pursue, then I want to go do something that is challenging, that I love, and that my heart's been in since I was a four-year-old boy, and that's pursuing the game of baseball."

His demeanor was inquisitive and calm, as if he knew no worry. He described to me how he maintained that physique. It was an equation that was part diet, part gumption, and part faith. A dormant brick pizza oven rested behind him. There was a pan inside, but I figured it was just for show. The oven didn't appear to have ever been used.

Unique ingredients were strewn about the countertop between us, including butter from grass-fed cows, something in a dropper called medium-chain triglyceride oil, coconut oil, organic whipping cream, almond milk, and the sweetener stevia. They were grouped together like a football huddle and flanked a piping-hot casserole pan that contained a breakfast dish comprising a dozen eggs, cheese, and organic sausage, and topped with crushed-up cashew nuts. (Bread was not welcome there.)

A bowl of guacamole rested beside an uncut avocado. (Good fat bolsters cognitive function.) An adjacent table hosted yet another bowl, this one spilling over with unshaven ginger root. (Great for digestive health.)

Tebow handed me a red mug of black coffee, pointed to the ingredients on the counter, and told me to mix them in. As I did so, a splash here and a drop there, he detailed the merits of the concoction, bulletproof coffee, claiming it had enough nutrients and calories to serve as breakfast. I tasted it. It was delicious. Around that same moment, Tebow's neighbor, then Washington Nationals second baseman Daniel Murphy, walked in.

Murphy is one of the most consistent hitters in Major League Baseball history, and he had invested in mentoring Tebow on the diamond, spending hours deconstructing raw athleticism and building it into a productive, strategic offensive weapon. That challenge, Murphy and Tebow said, was as much philosophical as it was physical.

From childhood, baseball players are taught to hit the center of the baseball up, resulting in line drives and ground balls. Make the defense work. Keep the ball out of the air. Ten years into his professional career, Murphy, at the behest of New York Mets hitting coach Kevin Long, shunned that philosophy, and passed that opposite approach on to Tebow. Murphy explained that someone with Tebow's raw gifts—namely, power—should want to hit the bottom half of the baseball. Hit it in the air. Strive for pop-ups during practice, because eventually those pop-ups would be honed into mortar launches beyond the outfield fence. And in today's professional baseball, power is currency.

"Daniel said, 'Look, your goal, with your power, is to be able to do damage,'" Tebow explained. "How do you do damage? You hit the ball far and you hit the ball high. So it was about breaking down barriers before I even started playing."

"We went and talked to some Little Leaguers, and my son was out there, he's about to be three, and I said, 'Where do we want them to hit the ball?'" Murphy adds. "He said, 'Hit it to the moon!' That's the thought. I want you to hit the ball over the moon."

That philosophy is apropos. Most give Tebow no shot at reaching the moon. He doesn't care. That's not his destination anyway. He's aimed at the stars.

"Don't tell him he can't do something! Trust me!" Murphy told me, laughing. "The passion and the excitement he brings to everything he does make everybody else take that same approach. I've honestly never seen it in baseball."

Football is a freight train. Baseball is a Greyhound bus.

The NFL season is sixteen games in length, all-out, all-the-time, unbridled intensity. That doesn't work in baseball. Baseball is 160-plus games, a long, slow grind from spring through the doldrums of summer and into the fall. That's when the intensity picks up in baseball, as the pennant races become clearer.

The respective mentalities required to sustain those seasons are quite different. Unless you're Tim Tebow.

"The way we tick as baseball players is like, it's just a really slow build," Murphy explained. "So to see him come in with all his energy, and his excitement, and all this passion, it got me excited.

"I usually don't really start trying to hit until the middle of January, because I know how long camp is and I know how long the season is. But he came in and he was so excited. It was cool to see an elite athlete make the kind of adjustments he made. I mean, his first professional at bat, it had been like a decade since he played. You went bridge!"

"Bridge" is baseball code for hitting a home run. On September 28, 2016, Tebow stepped into the batter's box on Field No. 6 in

St. Lucie, Florida, facing St. Louis Cardinals left-handed pitching prospect John Kilichowski, in his first plate appearance as a professional. He swung at the very first pitch Kilichowski threw. And he went yard.

"I loved that!" Murphy said. "I watched it on ESPN, and it was one of the most impressive things I've ever seen. Ever. To see the adjustments he makes and the passion that he brings on a daily basis—even in the dead of off-season—it was unique, and it gave me energy."

Murphy's explanation why was impeccable and precise.

"One of the coolest things that sparked our relationship was the idea that we play, we live, we serve for something greater than ourselves, which is Jesus Christ, perfect life and death on a cross for our lives," Murphy continued. "And, as I listen to him speak, there's so much freedom in what he's allowed to do because he understands what he's designed for, which is to give God glory, and then that frees him up to pursue baseball or football or whatever he wants with reckless abandon. There's so much freedom in that.

"There's freedom in being able to pursue that. There's freedom to be able to serve others. And so that was probably one of the first things that drew us to each other, that idea that this is what we do, it's not who we are.

"And it's such a fine line, I think even in my own life, looking up at the scoreboard and thinking that the numbers on the scoreboard define who I am as a person. But I'm a father, I'm a husband, I'm a baseball player, I'm a friend. The game doesn't define me personally. And it's still something I struggle with on a daily basis of trying to find my identity in other places."

I fight that every single day. And I mean it: Every. Day. I consciously work to make certain that my job isn't my identity. My kids don't care what I do. They care that I'm present and attentive.

But ego creeps in. And pride creeps in. And some days I cannot help it. I mentioned this to Tebow.

"But, Marty, if I find my identity in football then, man, when I was blessed to win championships or the Heisman or the run to the [NFL] playoffs, I would feel great about myself.

"But then, when I've gotten cut three times, traded once—pretty much four teams didn't want me—or to go through those lows, then my identity and who I was would've been shattered to nothing. You're not defined by what the rest of the world says about you. You're not defined by that breakup, or when you lost the job. You're not defined by what the kids that bullied you in middle school said about you.

"You're defined when God said, 'I love you, you're created for a purpose, you're fearfully and wonderfully made'—that defines you. Now I have real purpose. Now I have true identity."

I also have a penchant for being consumed by the residual pride that comes from someone else's lack of belief in my ability. When someone says I can't, it becomes an unyielding mission to prove dead wrong their lack of confidence in me. That's healthy. Here's the problem: I struggle to let it go even when I've succeeded in proving them wrong. That's weak. I mentioned this, too, to Tebow.

"You can have a chip to want to prove people wrong, but it's not your identity and who you are," he explained. "You see, I get to walk in that door and I get to be an uncle, I get to be a brother, I get to be a son, I get to hang with my family.

"We get to go and serve the rest of the world with our foundation and all the people we're ministering to, and so that chip that a lot of times consumes people with bitterness, frustration—all these things—I get to let it go. I get to go live the rest of my life free by grace, not worried about what other people are saying about me. Because what other people said about me, that doesn't define me."

"Beach Girl"

I run the Ocean City, New Jersey, boardwalk most mornings in the summertime. All the way out and all the way back. Five miles. Past the snaking lines of weekly renters at Brown's and Oves' to-go windows, waiting anxiously for hot donuts. Brace for the wind tunnel at Gardens Plaza. Some days when you're headed south it's like running into a brick wall. When you turn to head back north it catapults you like a slingshot. Continue beyond the scramblers and the pirate ships at Gillian's and Playland. Stop and salute during the flag-raising ceremony and the national anthem, a boardwalk ritual at the waterpark since 9/11. The air smells like curly fries and salt water. Wave at the boys at Manco & Manco Pizza and squeeze by the Port-O-Call Hotel pool. All the while dodging families crossing the boards from St. James Place all the way to Twenty-Third Street, clutching umbrellas and chairs, wagonfuls of rations in tow, to stake their beachfront claim for the day. Before 12 p.m., bikes are permitted on the boards. So from dawn to high noon, it's like Frogger up there. I've been the frog plenty of times. I've been the truck a bunch, too. Running is an important mental purge for me. Every bit as important as the physical fitness it provides.

I gain clarity on the grind. Even in the middle of Frogger.

Beach Girl

There's somethin' 'bout a girl on a bike at the beach...
Wind whippin' through her hair as she pedals to the beat...
Sun glistens off the frame of her Ray-Bans...
Shimmers off the sheen of her tan...

One...two...three...four...
No racing just pacing like a dance floor...
Beauty in her smile...
Music in her laugh...
Man I wish I could be more like that...

Chapter Six

Keep Your Money

I'm that guy in the cartoons with the angel on one shoulder and the devil on the other. I fight the devil every day. And I lean hard on that angel for backup and direction. If ever there was an individual with one-half of his mother's DNA and one-half of his father's, it's me.

I got it honest. Because Momma was an angel and Daddy wrestled demons.

Sounds like a country song.

Like a lot of guys, my relationship with my father was complicated. Nobody loved me more. That is unquestionable. But he was hard as hell on me. The potential he saw in me was a blessing and a curse for an impressionable, self-absorbed mind. The mountain of expectations he built before me seemed impossible to scale. It wasn't. At all. But it felt that way. Fortunately, I was pretty self-motivated.

Dad grew up the only child of Leo and Eunice Martin Smith, a pair of high school educators born during the Great Depression. I never knew my granddaddy. He died of Parkinson's disease when I was two years old. But my gran, now, she was around. She made it more than ninety-eight years on this earth, mainly because she was tougher than a two-dollar steak and ornery as an ox, *the* most hardheaded human being I've ever known.

She worked dawn to dusk on our family farm every day, well into her nineties, fingers gnarled and bent, fingernails always painted pink but most often chipped. She built fence lines and painted gates and used handheld clippers to chop down thistle bushes in the hayfield. She picked up rocks from the fields and moved them to the bed of Sinking Creek.

Her work ethic was unparalleled.

The Commonwealth of Virginia took her driver's license away at some point, and she could no longer cross the mountain at her leisure. That was the beginning of the end. The DMV stripped her purpose. She used to ease down Highway 460 between Newport and Christiansburg, seventeen miles each way, peeking through the gap between the black steering wheel and the blue dashboard of her truck. Highway 460 regulars knew her truck, a '75 Chevy, white top, blue bottom, and they kindly negotiated around it.

There was Mrs. Leo, the crown of her soiled sun hat all that could be seen as they passed by.

She often sat on a bucket or a box of nails to see out the windshield. Eunice was frugal. She was so tight she squeaked, and nobody—I mean nobody—questioned her. In the summertime she employed the high school boys around the area to throw hay, and when they walked through the gate of Craig Valley Farms they straightened it up. Yes, ma'am. No, ma'am. Thank you, ma'am. They did well, too: ten bucks an hour. And she wrote every single one of them a personal check right there on the spot, yellow paper with black print, her husband's name always atop the left corner and her signature shorthand-scribbled illegibly (to anyone but her) on the bottom right. She always made certain that my grandfather was present. She preferred to be addressed as

Mrs. Leo Smith. She wasn't into frills. She wore lipstick and pearls and clip-on earrings to church. Other than that, not much jewelry. She wore her thin gold wedding band until the day she died.

When she did die, in 2012, my sister, Stacy, and I were the only Smiths left to address the reception line. We stood there for four hours. It felt like the entire New River Valley showed up. My gran took tremendous pride in the 2,958 students she taught to type and "keep house" at Christiansburg High School. We heard that number often. Most of them had a hilarious tale to tell about Gran.

Gran had a difficult time raising my father. Dad had terrible asthma, and for years as a boy he sat up through long nights breathing with the assistance of a croup kettle and my grandmother's soothing. That eliminated his opportunity to play sports. Daddy was competitive as hell. I inherited that, too. My best childhood friend, Mark Vinson, a Major League Baseball athletic trainer these days, states openly that the only man he's ever met who is more competitive than me is the major league pitcher David Price.

Dad didn't often tell me how proud he was of my accomplishments. But he absolutely told everybody else within earshot—because they told me that he told them. They still tell me.

I never understood that approach, and in fact, I resented it—until I became a father. When I had a son, and suddenly had to guide a boy just like me, that approach became crystal clear—you love them *so much*, and you know what awaits them out there in the world, so you're demanding in your efforts to prepare them. It's a taxing balance. I wish Dad were here so I could tell him I understand now.

My parents showed up at every single game, in every single sport I ever played, from fourth grade on. And I played all of them. Eighth-grade basketball at 3:30 on a winter Wednesday afternoon in Princeton, West Virginia, Mom and Dad were there. American Legion Baseball, 7:30 at night in the dead of summer, mid-July, out in Covington, three hours from home, on a work night, with the pungent stench of a paper mill in the air, and Mom and Dad were there, Daddy covered in dirt and grease, having come straight from the hayfield. High school football in the pouring rain deep in the coalfields of Haysi, Virginia, muddy and miserable, too cold for sanity, Mom and Dad were there. And they were there three hours before kickoff. The top bleacher on the 50-yard line was Dad's, everywhere we went.

Daddy lived it. He used to scream at the referees and the umpires. I don't mean complain; I mean scream. At them. Loudly. He once pulled out his money clip at Grayson County High School and waved it at a basketball referee. This is high school basketball in Nowhere, Virginia! His antics were well known around the area, and I was often mocked for it by rivals against whom I played. But I didn't care.

It was my dad, and if you came at me about my dad, you'd better be ready to fight. Because I was ready to fight.

His presence in those bleachers was a catalyst for my self-confidence. When you're young, you just want to know that Mom and Dad are watching. Mine were always watching. I will forever appreciate them for that commitment. Dad would later tell me he played vicariously through me, and when I went off to college the void he felt was immeasurable. I don't believe he ever shook the depression he experienced.

I haven't played an organized sport since 1995. But I still feel that presence in those bleachers.

Daddy died in 2008. It rocked me.

No matter what your relationship is with your dad, assuming you have any relationship at all, he provides a compass. He always seems to have the right answer when you're stumped and the right direction when you're lost. Roof's leaking? Call Daddy. Truck won't start? Call Daddy. Drove a hundred miles the wrong direction up

Interstate 81, all the way from Roanoke to Harrisonburg? Stop and call Daddy.

He'll just chuckle and tell you to fill up the tank before you turn around. Use the credit card, he'll say. Daddy will pay for it. Daddy paid for a lot of my screwups.

When I was in high school he taught me an unforgettable lesson about honesty. I swore he was going to kill me. I was seventeen, thought I had life figured, and he bought a brand-new white four-wheel-drive Ford F-150 from the Newberry Ford showroom floor. It was the fourth truck he'd owned in my lifetime, but by far the nicest, the first full-size and with self-locking hubs to boot.

Eight years before this, in 1985, he and his best friend, Gordon Jones, had painted the interior of our home. Gordon is a soothsayer and a genius, a man's man who can fix anything, who is one with the land and can predict weather events to the minute better than any trained meteorologist, and who chews Red Man tobacco and hangs a .22 and a 12 gauge behind his head in the back glass of his own Ford. I know it was '85 because of *Monday Night Football*. I was infatuated with the Chicago Bears that year, the characters and the swagger; they made defense cool, and they played the Green Bay Packers on TV as Daddy and Gordon painted those walls and drank a few Old Milwaukee beers.

When they finished, they simply carried the leftover paint cans downstairs to the basement and left them there. Those cans didn't move for nearly a decade, until eventually Momma wanted them gone, which, naturally, meant Daddy suddenly wanted them gone.

Lesson time. I woke up one Saturday morning to a note from Daddy: "Go downstairs and take the paint cans to the dump. Truck keys are on the counter." Seemed easy enough, *and* it meant I got to drive Daddy's new Ford. He'd built custom bed rails, painted them black, slapped a Spartan football sticker on the back glass, and used a black Sharpie to draw my jersey number, 9, into the center of the winged white football. The tires still had knobbies on the walls it was so new. The engine may have turned a couple hundred miles. Maybe.

I lined the truck bed with paint cans, maybe eight or ten of them, and took off down the highway. When I got to the dump I pulled up alongside a series of large green trash receptacles, and realized I was close enough to toss the cans directly from the truck bed into the bins. That worked perfectly. Until it didn't.

You know how paint cans have that thin wire handle? In the upswing toward the receptacle on one of those paint can tosses, that thin wire handle got hung up on my middle finger, shooting the can straight up into the air, and straight down—flush—onto the pavement. The lid blew off the can and beige paint splattered all the way down the passenger side of my daddy's white Ford truck. How in the name of Sherwin-Williams that paint was not dried up is a marvel of science and almost certainly marked the end of my life.

I freaked out, ripped off my shirt, and started wiping and cussing. Once my shirt was covered my shorts came off. Once my shorts were covered I went to my socks. You get the idea. It didn't look like that much paint, but it seemed to multiply. The more I wiped, the more immune to fabric absorption it seemed. Eventually I was out of clothes, but I felt pretty good about how the truck looked.

I drove home and walked into the house. Daddy was on the couch, just inside the door. He was perplexed as to why I was half naked. I got some pants and we walked back outside. I told him what had happened and expressed my deepest apologies for defacing his prized pickup. He looked at me. I braced for impact. He looked back at the truck. He inhaled a Marlboro Light. He looked back at me. It was the moment of truth.

He kicked the right-rear fender. Like, waylaid it, kicked a dent right there in the damn fender.

"Aw, hell. It's just a farm truck anyway, buddy. It's okay. Put some damn clothes on."

He walked back into the house and never said another word about it. That was it! I was alive! Half naked and in some level of shock, but alive! I'd hope to have that reaction if my son did anything that stupid, especially when born from laziness. I highly doubt I would.

Daddy's favor was the ultimate endorsement because it was not readily known.

Mom's favor, meanwhile, was known, felt, seen, heard, and embraced. It was even eaten, when she awoke early on Saturday morning to bake those orange-flavored Pillsbury sweet rolls just because Stacy and I loved them so much, and she loved us so much, and she loved our reaction when we woke up to that smell.

She would stay up well past her usual bedtime to make my favorite birthday cake—homemade, from scratch, chocolate lathered in homemade, from scratch, white buttercream icing. I used to sneak slices for breakfast, after practice, before dinner, after dinner, thinking she wouldn't notice. In one day it was nearly gone. Dummy.

Everyone adored my mother, Joy. She was the most gracious person I've ever known. She *was* grace. Choir director at the church. Pep rally organizer. Halloween costume designer. Tulip grower and pruner, her flowers red and yellow, tall and lush and flawless, lining the front porch bed. Voracious reader, Clancy and Grisham and Grizzard. Lewis Grizzard made my parents snort in laughter. They used to quote him at the dinner table over beans and corn bread. One of their favorite books was *Shoot Low, Boys— They're Ridin' Shetland Ponies*. Mom and Dad would say random lines aloud and howl at each other, and my sister and I would exchange looks, eat a spoonful of beans, and shrug.

Joy was the team mom on every one of my teams. Most of my

buddies considered her their second mom. She painted my number on her cheek and wore my jersey. She just had an innate kindness that welcomed all comers.

On May 24, 1998, Mom died. Breast cancer. She was forty-seven years old. I was barely twenty-two. One of my life's greatest regrets was choosing not to spend more time with her while she was sick. I was young and self-centered, a college senior, career-driven, focused on big dreams and raising hell with my buddies on the weekends. I didn't really grasp the finality of her illness. Youth defies the understanding of death. With time we glean perspective on our fragility.

Life is so precious, but I couldn't rationalize that until I was older. I'll never forgive myself for that.

Lainie will tell you that Mom urged me not to come home, urged me to spend time at school with her and my friends. That may be true. But I hate myself for listening to her. Because I know she would have loved to spend that time with me.

When Mom died, Daddy died. His soul did, anyway. He hung around physically for another ten years, but he was emotionally empty, angry, depressed, and bitter as a winter wind. He gave up on most things, and he spent most of his time in a beige leather recliner in the den, with three fingers of Crown Royal and two packs of Marlboro Lights and a mountain of Ho Hos.

My father was a brilliant man, a numbers guy with a calculator mind, who used that talent to put himself through college and ultimately, by his early forties, rise to a chief financial officer position at the local plastics plant, called Xaloy.

He did well financially, and he was very generous to the community—especially my high school athletic teams. If we had a road trip, it wasn't uncommon for him to pick up the McDonald's tab for the entire team. Once, during a football playoff trip to the coalfields, we stopped at the Western Steer—which to us may as well have been Morton's—and Dad bought steak dinners for every player and coach in the program. It must have been seventy-five people. I always appreciated that. I hope I told him so.

For those ten years after Mom died, he smoked one Marlboro off the next, to the point that the entire house smelled like stale smoke and the walls and windows were soiled by nicotine tar as thick and as yellow as pollen.

When he died in April 2008, he left me with six figures of credit card debt to settle and a childhood home so dilapidated it was condemnable. It pissed me off. But I wouldn't let that home go. It held my little-boy dreams, from the foul-line dunks on the shower curtain to the Lane Stadium leaps over the goal line "pile"—the arm of the couch—and onto the cushions.

Those walls heard every childhood dream I ever had.

We moved to Pearisburg in 1980, when I was four years old. On the drive from Salem, West Virginia, to Pearisburg during our move, Momma hit an ice patch in her little sky-blue sedan, and the car spun around 360 degrees. Mom was horrified and my sister was bawling. I brought some levity, exclaiming that it was the most awesome thing I'd ever experienced, "like the Dukes of Hazzard, Momma!" Mom told that story often.

I used to go back home to Pearisburg to work on the house. It needed paint, flooring, a new deck, and a truckload of soap and weeks of elbow grease. Being there was a difficult brand of solitude, one that melded primal sorrow with hands-up futility, one in which memories danced the floor and, quite literally, hung on the walls, via unfortunate Olan Mills family church portraits and the like, and in which emptiness hung in the air.

I felt so alone there.

The whole exercise of cleaning out the house was emotionally exhausting. It troubled me. It still troubles me. I'm not sure why.

I'm not proud of it, but I'd drink enough Jack Daniel's to tranquilize a moose. And I'd hit the repeat button on the compact disc machine. The Eric Church album *Sinners Like Me* would play on a loop, full tilt, as loud as I could crank it. The music provided the perfect vehicle to carry my emotions in the moment.

That sounds like a country song. The best country songs are nonfiction.

Most times I was alone. And most of the time I was in the den.

The floor was disgusting, faux wood linoleum, cracked and soiled with sporadic patches of black goo. I don't know what that goo was, but it pissed me off.

That floor was a symbol of my parents' progress. It was laid atop what was once a concrete-slab carport, garnished with embedded oil stains. They converted it to the den when I was in seventh grade, and our 900-square-foot brick home expanded to 1,000. Mom kept it white-glove spotless, always.

Seated on that floor, over to my right, cigarette burns stippled the armrests on Daddy's chair. He'd fall asleep sometimes after a long week, watching *Jeopardy!* or Dan Rather or *60 Minutes* or another History Channel Vietnam documentary, or get fired up watching Virginia Tech play football on a Saturday afternoon, and the Marlboro Light in his left hand would scorch that thing. Black circles.

I felt like a king in that chair, up high in Dad's lap and within his aura. He had quite an aura. His attention was mine in that chair. His passions were my passions in that chair.

He was a god.

And it was in that chair that I learned the true depth of my parents' generosity. It was in the summer, maybe July, and I was in the house alone trying to make some progress on the cleanup. Suddenly the lawn began to fill up with trucks and cars. Several of my high school football teammates had learned that I was in town and refused to let me be alone, so they stopped by with a couple of cases of beer to share some old laughs and tell some old lies.

It was a wonderful surprise. During this time, I recalled that I owed two of them, twin brothers Anthony and Aaron Myers, a lot of money. They owned a landscaping business, Weed Whackers they called it, and I'd hired them to do extensive work to the exterior of the house. I hadn't paid them.

So in the middle of the party, I got up, grabbed the checkbook, and asked Anthony how much I owed them. He told me to put my money away. I refused and asked the question again. He again told me to put my money away. I sat down and started to write a check, and Anthony stood up, slammed his hand down on the checkbook, and said in a raised voice: "I told you...put your damn money away."

Then he explained himself. Anthony and Aaron had a tough upbringing. Their mother was a single mom, and she worked her fingers to the bone at a convenience store to keep clothes on the boys' backs and their bottomless bellies full. Aaron later explained to me that they required government assistance, and that their father lived close by but was not involved in their lives. Many nights, Aaron told me, dinner consisted of a pack of nabs and a Mountain Dew. That was it. Crackers and soda. When they were boys their older brother, Chris, was stabbed to death following a dispute at a party. Their mother would never feel whole again.

The Myers twins were rough kids and fought for what they got. But they were loyal as a guard dog to those who paid them respect. Still are. And the Smiths were loyal.

My mother adored them both. I'd often see her hugging them in the hallway at school pep rallies, reminding them that they were loved, and loved by many. Anthony, specifically, was like a younger brother to me. When I graduated from school and left town, he inherited my football jersey number: 9. To this day when I see him, he calls me "Niner." It's been way too long since I've seen him.

After he hollered at me to put away my money, Anthony sat back down on the couch beside me and explained why he didn't want it. He explained that there were many days during our youth that had Momma not handed lunch money to Aaron and him, they wouldn't have eaten that day.

That comment stopped time.

It was a revelation to me. Mom never told anyone.

She just did what was right.

And I folded myself into Daddy's chair and buried my head in a puddle of sorrow. I've rarely cried that hard in my life. And I'd never seen Anthony Myers cry. Until then. He melted, too, right into me. And we hugged hard for several minutes.

I was so proud of my parents in that moment. I was so proud of my last name.

Because right then the definition of my last name was "humble and kind."

And I know my parents smiled.

Chapter Seven

Dirty 'Merica

We had seven minutes.

The boys and I were in China, speeding from Shanghai to Beijing in a minivan stuffed to capacity, our bodies contorted into crevices between windows and boxes upon boxes of television gear—and other bodies—hustling to attend an event with the global soccer icon Cristiano Ronaldo. We'd been in China with Ronaldo for several days, chasing this mysterious, untouchable legend in an effort to produce a lengthy television feature.

We'd never met him. But he warmed to us quickly—in part because it was warm. Very warm.

On the first day in Shanghai we were to capture a wide-ranging "sit-down" interview, which we had planned to open at the Peninsula Hotel at 2 p.m., on a gorgeous veranda overlooking the Bund, with the stunning Shanghai cityscape behind us, just across the Huangpu River.

But it was sweltering. In fact, it was the hottest day on record in Shanghai in 145 years. The iPhone thermometer displayed 108 degrees. Records indicate it was 106. So when Ronaldo arrived in the hotel suite and walked out to the veranda, my cameraman, Gregg

Hoerdemann, hit record immediately, and I quickly addressed his camera:

It's one of the great honors of my life to interview the most famous athlete on the planet, Cristiano Ronaldo, and we had planned to begin our chat out here with the beautiful Shanghai cityscape behind us. But it's 108 degrees, so the hell with that.

Ronaldo, stunned but amused, responded, "Yeah, [beep] that." In we went.

Days later we're in that minivan again, zipping through the remote Chinese countryside, debating whether or not we should stop at the Great Wall of China. Do we have time? If we don't stop, will we regret it forever? This is a one-shot chance, boys. It's highly likely we'll never be in China again.

Let's roll.

We threw the van in park and checked the time. We had to hurry. Getting to the Great Wall of China from the parking lot is much more involved than you might imagine. You walk up a steep hill—it was damn near Everest as I recall it—to a ski lift, which carts you up the mountain to the Wall. We didn't have time to walk. We ran. Straight up that mountain.

It required a team effort. Standard job responsibilities did not apply. Egos, neither. Time was precious. The producer threw a heavy tripod across his shoulders and took off. Just took off, full bore, up that hill. One of the members of my camera team lugged a cumbersome Ronin camera rig as he scurried up the hill. I just ran, dodging folks coming back down the hill the entire time. When we got in the ski lift pod, my producer, a neurotic keep-to-the-schedule planner, determined we had less than ten minutes.

When we hopped out, he yelled, *"Seven minutes!"*

The camera crew, Gregg and Sam Hoerdemann, father and son, made quick work, capturing the incredible beauty and commanding presence of the Great Wall, its twists and turns and unique character, its undulations and architecture, its history. The day was hot but overcast, providing enviable lighting. People were everywhere and from everywhere.

Gregg and Sam managed, within minutes, to capture the essence of one of the earth's true wonders. The Great Wall was built centuries ago by the hands of more than a million men. It stretches more than thirteen thousand miles across northern China.

One older man was dressed as an ancient Chinese warrior; he had donned a golden helmet capped with a red feather, a beautiful golden suit of armor with red flowy sleeves and golden armored cuffs, shoulder plates, and chest and loin coverage, which was secured by a bronze belt depicting a face with a ring through its mouth. And he carried a massive silver sword, with a red tassel dangling from a thick, black handle.

Gregg, whom I believe can peer through a viewfinder and directly into a soul, gestured to the man to unsheathe the weapon. The warrior gladly did so. And as he did so, his eyes suggested a sense of accomplishment.

I wondered if his eyes flashed pride in displaying his heritage.

Time was up. And there was no debating the clock.

We had to board that ski lift back down the mountain. And if we didn't go just then, we'd be late for Ronaldo's arrival in Beijing. Or worse yet, miss him altogether. But when we got in line we realized we had a serious problem.

There must have been five hundred people in that line, winding—idle, mind you—from the ski lift entrance all the way back up to the platform entrance to the Great Wall.

We deliberated for a brief moment. Then the producer, Jonathan

Whyley, spoke a ten-word sentence we will never forget: "Boys, listen… It's time to go dirty 'Merica on 'em."

No one questioned what that meant.

We all knew.

We lined up and snaked around and through and between whatever was in our way, down the path and past the line. We balanced down the rock border along the path. We bobbed. We weaved. We slithered.

Once we made our way down the winding rock staircase to the platform entrance of the lift, our opportunity to pass by the line ended. We had to cut line now. There were barriers installed that created a chute of sorts to direct visitors toward the lift entrance. Dammit. We were stuck.

Then Jonathan yelled something about being moments away from "live."

Without a word, Gregg and Sam threw their cameras up on their shoulders and pointed them directly at me. And turned them on. When the red light is on, it's go-time.

I began addressing those cameras—as if we were capturing live video for television. And we walked through the crowd, toward the ski lift entrance, and I just kept talking and talking.

"You cannot fathom the beauty of the Great Wall of China. Built hundreds of years ago by more than a million men, stretching longer than half the earth's equator…"

Just talking straight out my ass.

Whatever came to mind, I said. When I ran out of ideas, Jonathan barked directions. Gregg stared through the lens. Sam shot ornate moments of my drivel and nothingness.

The crowd parted.

They took photographs of us. They reached for us.

It was unbelievable.

When we arrived at the entrance door, I grabbed the handle in an attempt to exit through the entrance. It was locked. We really were stuck this time.

Then, suddenly, a man near the front of the line in a black suit with a white shirt and a red tie said, "Americans? I'll help!" And he excused himself past the folks in front of him, scooched to the front of the line, leaned around the silver partition separating the entrance door from the exit door, and unlocked the entrance door!

And we walked right through, straight to the next open ski lift pod. But not before we turned back and grabbed the man who had opened the door for us, and asked him to come with us. He was Afghani and his name was Alaam. And he was wonderful and kind and absolutely hilarious. We thanked him effusively and we laughed with him and we asked him to take a photograph with us. He had a beautiful laugh and a warm smile.

Weeks later, when our Chinese adventure with Ronaldo aired on ESPN and the credits rolled, they scrolled atop that photograph of us with Alaam. And the very last thank-you in those credits was sincere appreciation to Alaam.

Because of him, we kept to that meticulous schedule.

And we were on time for Ronaldo.

And "Dirty 'Merica" became legend. For us, anyway.

Chapter Eight

Girl Power

Dale Earnhardt Jr. could hardly walk. For weeks he could barely stand when he woke up. And it wasn't getting any better. He was terribly discouraged and downright scared.

It was September 2016, and life as Earnhardt had previously known it was a distant memory. For more than a decade he'd been the most popular racing driver in America. But in that moment, as every step felt like a mile, cumbersome and laborious and awkward, the only thing racing was his mind.

He worried desperately about the future and obsessed about his injured brain. Would it still protect and project the sweet memories from days past once he emerged from this sluggish aftermath? Would he even emerge from the aftermath? Would he ever again live a life that resembled being functional?

Months prior, in early July, Earnhardt had finished thirteenth in the NASCAR Cup Series race at the Kentucky Speedway. He hadn't been in a race car since. During that weekend in Sparta, Kentucky, he began to feel mentally aloof and distant, almost like he had the space-cadet beginnings of a sinus infection. After consulting with doctors, it was determined that he was experiencing delayed symptoms from a concussion, suffered weeks before in a wreck during a race at the Michigan Speedway.

It was his third recorded concussion and would ultimately rewrite his future.

This time his balance and vision suffered dramatically. If you race automobiles for a living, no two physical attributes are more important.

Earnhardt required assistance to get from the bedside to the bathroom. His eyes divorced each other, no longer a couple working in unison, unable to coexist even with therapy. He couldn't linger in dimly lit rooms and couldn't see in well-lit ones. Dark rooms compromised his spatial awareness and made him dizzy. And dizziness made him nauseous. In daylight his eyes wouldn't focus.

Meanwhile, his mind couldn't seem to focus anywhere. As a racing driver, lack of focus was foreign. Racing drivers have heightened instincts and quicker-than-average reaction times. At 200 miles per hour, life comes at you quickly. Racing drivers have peripheral vision fields spanning greater than 180 degrees, widened by repetition during competition. Survival of the fittest. Adapt and improve or you won't be around very long.

Repetition elevates a race car driver's senses to nearly clairvoyant anticipatory levels. See it before it happens—or it happens to you. That used to be Earnhardt's normal. And now here he was, struggling to stand, to see, and to maintain everyday conversations of any appreciable length.

Relationships suffered. Countless obligations were placed on hold. For that matter, everything in his life was placed on hold—except his relationship with his fiancée, Amy Reimann. At the time Earnhardt was integrated into dozens of long-term planning projects, from helping develop Chevrolet's newest NASCAR race car model, to the day-to-day operations of his own racing team,

JR Motorsports, to daily sponsorship obligations for his many team and personal corporate partners.

He had to completely remove himself. For five months he unplugged. Friends, peers, and colleagues couldn't understand why he didn't respond to texts or emails or why he wouldn't call them back. They wondered why he acted as though they no longer existed. Explaining why was futile. He looked fine. So what was the problem?

The truth was, he was just trying to exist. There was no way for most people, even some of his closest confidants and family members, to comprehend or respect the extent of the postconcussion symptoms that rewrote Junior's normal, altered his perspective, and ended up changing his life forever.

Amy understood. She walked every step with him. During their seven-year relationship, she meticulously chipped away at Junior's stubborn emotional walls, built within Earnhardt over time by heartache and insecurity and the chase for something tangible to which he might cling. Those walls caged his potential.

Amy taught him how to be vulnerable. He would never be more vulnerable than this.

"He felt helpless," Amy told me. "It terrified him and it terrified me. Helpless is a hard thing to watch."

Junior called his neurologist—University of Pittsburgh concussion expert Dr. Micky Collins—at all hours of the day and night, plumb wore him out, concerned that this merciless condition was permanent.

"Nothing's changing, right? And so I'm talking to Micky in the middle of the night, because I'm scared to damn death, because nothing's getting any better," Earnhardt told me. "I'm telling [Collins], don't feed me no BS, man. Am I at risk to carry this with me?

"Is this going to change at all? Have you seen this before?

Have you seen guys with the same symptoms walk in and go, 'I'm healed! I'm 100 percent!'? I was just so scared."

Discussing this, Earnhardt was seated alongside Amy, now his new bride of twenty-eight days, on a silver barstool with a glittery, sparkly red cushion like you'd find at an old '60s ice-cream parlor. It was positioned in the center of the shop floor of his personal storage space/race shop/basketball court/lounging area/man cave/rehab center on the grounds of Dirty Mo Acres, his sprawling 130-acre compound forty miles north of Charlotte, North Carolina.

We convened on a cold January morning to discuss the hell through which they'd both trudged, and the heaven they'd found along the way.

"I get so frustrated trying to explain it, because there's no way I can help someone who's never had a concussion, never went through it, understand what it's like," he said. "Because you can look at the person, and there's no wound or injury you can physically see, or tangibly touch. Everyone had to be really patient with something they couldn't see or touch or understand."

Dr. Collins always managed to calm Junior's fears, and he suggested Earnhardt wholly commit to performing daily balance and vision correction exercises. Collins stressed that recovery times varied by individual, and could span from three weeks to three years, depending on the person. No two concussions and no two brains are identical.

Concussions are like snowflakes. From a distance they all look the same. But when studied closely, they're all intricate and unique, their details one of a kind. That makes their respective recovery times and tactics equally intricate and unique. Collins had seen cases with similar symptoms to Earnhardt's, and he had cured them.

At Amy's urging, Junior was indeed diligent during rehab. Per

Dr. Collins's direction, he turned his competitiveness on the racetrack toward recovery techniques that melded balance and vision. In one session he might stand on a BOSU ball while visually chasing specific light marks on the wall.

Another session might involve performing individual basketball drills that include changes of direction. He performed plyometric movements, including box jumps and burpees that required pitching and catching medicine balls to simultaneously activate reaction time and core strength.

He performed vision rehabilitation exercises with tiny eye charts, which he held one foot from his face, and walked backward and forward in ten-foot-long paths, shaking his head back and forth at 150 beats per minute, while staring at the eye chart to locate specific letters in a jumbled display. The most challenging aspect of his visual recovery involved a disco light in a dark room. Earnhardt walked backward and forward while moving his head from left to right, focused on various light patterns bouncing across the wall.

One of the final rehab practices he performed each day was a 3-D program on his laptop called Visual Performance Enhancement. For twenty-five minutes he wore sunglasses, specifically developed for the computer program, that forced his eyes to cross, and thereby retrained them to work in unison, which Earnhardt badly needed. Since it was internet-based, Collins and his team could see Junior's results in real time.

He also had to relearn how to interact in society. The bustle of public places made him extremely anxious. So Collins instructed Earnhardt to go to busy places like the grocery store and interact. These are called "exposure" techniques, which deliberately triggered his symptoms.

By October 2016 he was back at the racetrack, visiting old friends. His symptoms and his outlook were vastly improved. Now that he was on the mend, life was just a bit sweeter than before, his perspective redefined. It was a long, scary road. Amy held his compass.

Without Amy, I don't believe Dale would have recovered quite so well or quite so quickly. Without her, I don't know that he'd have had the necessary level of confidence or diligence. Before he met her, his confidence was defined by the performance of his race car. And during concussion recovery he had no race car.

She rode his ass. She's the first—and remains the only—person I've ever met who could ride his ass and get results.

I've known Earnhardt for half our lives. We've been pretty good buddies for most of that time. These days I consider him to be one of my trusted friends, more like a brother. We don't talk every day. But I know he genuinely wants the very best for me, and I hope he knows I want the very best for him, and that my intentions are always true.

We have history. We've walked through some real hard times together, taken different roads to similar brands of happiness. Losing parents too soon is a side street on that journey. Granted, my parents weren't famous. I had to remind him of that once.

In the spring of 2008, I wrote a cover piece for *ESPN The Magazine* on Junior's decision to leave the racing company his father founded, Dale Earnhardt, Inc., to go drive for the New York Yankees of NASCAR—Hendrick Motorsports. It was a seismic decision in the motorsports world.

It meant Junior would leave a bunch of good ol' boys, representing blue-collar companies like Budweiser and Bass Pro Shops, to team with a bunch of pretty boys, Jeff Gordon and Jimmie Johnson, in the Hendrick stable, thereby adding to the superteam's already bountiful cupboard. Junior had always been a rebel, unrefined and unbridled and untucked, the antithesis of the tucked-in white oxford Hendrick brand.

His decision to join them was viewed by many fans as treason.

During the interview for that *Magazine* piece, the topic arose that my father was ill. Seated on barstools at a dusty countertop in the go-kart service bay of the Union 76 gas station on his property, between pulls off a couple of those Budweiser beers, we started talking about our dads.

We both idolize our dads. Present tense. Not past. Our dads drove our passions. (In Junior's case, quite literally.) But we likewise adore our mothers, and we're smart enough to know that our moms are the knots in the ties that bind us.

He asked me how I carried on after losing my mom. We'd never discussed this before. I told him I was still working on it. He considered that answer for a minute, and appreciated my understanding of the element of time in the grieving process. (When a loved one dies, I always maintain that time is the only respite. But even time will fail you more often than not.)

I reminded Junior that I couldn't understand *his* element. My hurt was just for my family and me. Insular. He had to shoulder the sorrow of millions of No. 3 fans and the weight of the entire NASCAR industry. Millions of people, including thousands of men and women who earn their keep in the NASCAR garage every week, looked directly to Junior for light in the darkness, and for permission to forge on.

Superman doesn't die. And for legions of passionate fans, Dale Earnhardt was part Superman, part John Wayne, and part Elvis. Dale Jr.'s sister Kelley once explained to me that for years the Earnhardt kids didn't have the opportunity to grieve their father's death. Fans would approach them daily in the checkout line and at the gas pump to detail their own personal sorrow, never stopping to consider the pain and emptiness the Earnhardt kids must have felt.

Junior and I both yearned to earn our fathers' favor, and we didn't always feel adequate. During that *Magazine* interview, I asked him to share a story that he felt best encapsulated his relationship with his dad. He told me a story about a bucket. Here is an excerpt from that piece, dated May 9, 2008:

The paint bucket sat across the shop floor, and Dale Earnhardt ordered his kid to pick it up. It was bulky, the five-gallon kind, weighing every bit as much as the boy. Dale Earnhardt Jr. had no hope of picking it up, and he knew it, so the 8-year-old moped across the floor, questioning his old man's direction: How could Daddy ask this? Why does he gotta make me feel bad?

Daddy despised reluctance, especially from blood, and certainly from the boy who bore his name.

Dale Earnhardt—Ironhead, The Intimidator—had built a life, and ultimately a legend, on will. He was raised by a stock car pioneer, Ralph Earnhardt, at a time when even the best drivers raced to put food on the table. Ralph had worked his way through the textile mill and manhandled a hundred secondhand race cars around a hundred crappy little race tracks. So Dale's kids sure as hell weren't about to get off easy. When Dale Jr. did anything less than attack that bucket and grab it by the handle, his father found another way to motivate: He asked a shop hand to move it—right in front of his son.

"The lesson was to try it," Junior says. "Instead of being a quitter and not even attempting it, you should have tried. That was Daddy telling me that. If I can't pick it up, drag it across the floor. But I didn't even go over there to try, and he'd get so disappointed in me for being such a cop-out. Daddy would've been the kind of kid who walked over there and tried to pick it up, without a word. I should've been more like that. And I should be more like that today."

We're honest with each other, even when honesty requires criticism. Once, in 2012, Junior taught me a lesson—quite probably the most influential advice I've ever received about my occupation: Shut up and listen.

I had conducted an interview with Jeff Gordon weeks before, during which I had interrupted him multiple times to ensure the first-ballot NASCAR Hall of Fame driver didn't talk around specific questions and stayed on-task. The interview aired on ESPN's *NASCAR Countdown* program prior to a Cup Series race in Loudon, New Hampshire.

After the race that day, I was charged with finding Earnhardt for comment on his performance. He exited the driver's window of his car, surveyed the cosmetic damage, and signaled for me to join him on the trailer lift gate of his team's 18-wheeler before he addressed the larger media scrum.

He turned his back to the assemblage, looked up at me, and told me to shut up. Right to my face—"Man, you need to stop interrupting people."

I was confused. He laid into me pretty good, more demonstrative than normal. He wanted to hear Gordon's extended thoughts on certain topics, and I'd disallowed some detail and context because I didn't let the interview breathe. I was embarrassed. But I knew Dale was right. I knew I had let the desire to prove myself drive the conversation with Gordon. Junior's advice completely altered my philosophical approach to interviewing people. And as a result I improved markedly.

In 2009 Earnhardt was competitively awful. It depressed him. He was so bad, few folks believed he'd ever win again. That included him. He told me he was stealing other drivers' opportunities on the racetrack, filling the seat of a race car someone else deserved. He wouldn't look anyone in the eye. He was emotionally fragile and embarrassed. I constantly told him it would get better, and to get his head up off his chest and look at people, because improvement was coming. I didn't sense he appreciated my thoughts.

Nothing seemed to help. Except Amy.

If there has ever been an example of the transformative power of love, it is Dale Earnhardt Jr. I've never met or seen anyone more profoundly and fundamentally impacted by love's vulnerability than him. With Earnhardt, there's Before Amy and After Amy.

They met in 2008, when she sat across from him at a boardroom table. She was part of an interior design group that would decorate Earnhardt's new home. He was instantly smitten. She was smart and confident and witty. And she was the most beautiful thing he'd ever seen. She was also married.

And she didn't know who he was, either, other than that he was the shy client who wanted belt buckles hung on the wall. Eventually she separated from her former husband, and in time she and Junior started dating. Before they met, Earnhardt was a hell-raiser of legendary proportions. He drank and caroused and carried on. He was also reclusive. He didn't go out in public much, choosing instead to host friends at his property and subconsciously build up even more physical and emotional barriers to the outside world. In many ways he was isolated. Even with all those people raising all that hell around him, he often felt alone.

"When you're by yourself, you're your own cheerleader—and sometimes it's hard to cheer," Junior told me. "Sometimes when you feel defeated or you feel down, that cheerleader inside you didn't get the job done. So you make a lot of decisions, basically, on your own.

"And these are everyday personal decisions on how to handle a disagreement with someone you love, or how to patch up a disagreement, little simple things that involve your morals and values. And being young and naive and immature, I wasn't always making the right choices. I didn't always handle every situation the right way.

"But when you have someone that you trust, believe in, that you spend so much time with and who gets to know you so well, she can see me coming a mile away no matter what. No matter what I'm thinking or doing, she knows it, and I have someone to cheer for me, someone to tell me to get off the floor when I get knocked down—or somebody to tell me I was wrong.

"She's got such a perspective that I don't have. And she can really be honest with me. She'll tell me the truth no matter what the truth is."

I asked Amy about hangers-on and enablers, and whether she believed Dale Jr. had too many of both.

"I had a sense of normalcy, I think, that he never knew before," Amy explained. "I didn't have anybody telling me yes just because of who I was. The majority of people around him when we met were yes-men. A lot of his friends were just around for the fun and out for the party. So most of the people that were yes-people were those people.

"I wouldn't say his family members necessarily do that, they hold him pretty accountable. So it's mostly just friends—and they're not really around anymore."

As their relationship developed, Amy told me Junior became much more caring and compassionate and thoughtful of others, and more considerate of who he included and who he didn't, and why. He became more selective about relationships in which he invested, and more focused on enriching those selected.

And he became noticeably happier.

"Amy changed my life," Junior told me. "She really stuck with me through a lot of years, and I changed as a person. She's a huge part of that. And I went from being very selfish and self-centered, and only about what was good for me and what I wanted to do in that moment, and have grown to be more considerate, more caring, and much happier.

"With her, everything about my life is better. Every day there's something she does that surprises me, that reaffirms my belief that she loves me. There are things that a person does—genuine thoughts and emotions and actions, and I see that in her all the time. So I know where she's coming from is real.

"And she was with me in a lot of dark times, the concussions and just different things that I've struggled with most. Everybody has personal struggles. She's been there and she wants to be there. She insists on being there. Pretty incredible. Nobody's ever done that for me, been there every single moment.

"So I thought I'd be a complete idiot if I didn't ask her to marry me."

The proposal was like that from a fairy tale. For some time, Earnhardt had been researching his genealogy, and in June 2015 he took his family on a vacation to his ancestors' birthplace, Ilbesheim, Germany. They lodged in a quaint bed-and-breakfast and spent the first day touring the town. On the second day he led them to a church. This was the same church in which the Earnhardt ancestors actually worshipped hundreds of years before, and its pastor, who spoke no English, showed them around while one of Junior's friends translated from German to English.

During the tour Amy made her way to the altar, and when she turned around, Junior was staring at her "with that intense Earnhardt look on his face."

She wasn't sure why. And then Junior, nervous but confident, got down on one knee.

He'd watched her get ready that morning, and he knew the timing was perfect. He chose against planning any speeches. He'd stifled the surprise for months, and he wanted his words to be authentic to the moment.

"I had a hard time in that moment putting into words what Amy meant to me and why I was doing this," he said with a laugh. "It's hard to show her my appreciation for what she's meant to me and how it's helped my life. In that moment you want to say all those things, and you want to put it all out there and explain it, but it's best probably to go on and ask the question you're there to ask.

"So I fumbled around with a little speech trying to get my feelings out. And that was a bit of a funny moment, but it was great. She was shocked, blown away."

She immediately said yes, her hands over her face the entire time, trying to process this permanent step toward forever.

"It was just a great moment," Earnhardt said. "There was already a lot of emotion because we were connected to my heritage. And if you do all the work to get to that and understand what your family has been through for one hundred, two hundred, three hundred years, once you get into that place, that physical place where they were, it's quite incredible.

"So I had that going on, on top of knowing what I was going to do that day. When I got up in the morning, and I'm looking at her while she's getting ready, and she has no idea. I was thrilled she said she would marry me."

Juxtapose the euphoria in Germany with the fear in Carolina one year later, that he might not be able to stand up straight at the altar as his bride walked the aisle toward him. His initial request to Dr. Collins centered on that very moment.

"When I went in for the first evaluation, I said all I care is that when I get married I don't have any symptoms. I don't want a foggy brain not being able to remember anything," Earnhardt said. "I don't want to have balance issues or be worried about falling over, or stumbling over my own feet. I want my eyes to work right. And I want to be able to climb in a deer stand and not feel like I'm gonna fall out of the tree, and be able to pull my bow back, stand up and shoot a deer if possible. I just wanted to live.

"Just get me fixed, get me back to being a normal person. I'm scared I'm not going to be able to live my life the way I want to live it. And we want to have kids, and I don't want to have any limitations."

One thing he didn't care about was ever racing again.

"Racing put me in this position," he said bluntly. "The very first thing you think is, 'I'm never driving again.' And the reason you say that to yourself is because of how bad you feel, and because your eyes don't work, and because you can't stand up, and because you never want to be in that position again.

"And so your initial reaction is, 'I don't want to be like this. So I'm never doing that, to put myself in that position to be like this. Never again.'"

But time is a great equalizer. With time and healing and immersion back within the NASCAR garage and its culture, Junior got the itch. He knew he would. As he started to heal and began to see and think with clarity, he stressed to Amy, Kelley, and Dr. Collins that he would want to race again. He knew he'd have a difficult decision to make. He'd already lived this movie once, and he knew the ending. Years before, in 2012, he sat out two races late in the season with postconcussion symptoms. They weren't nearly as dramatic as the 2016 episode, but they were most certainly a glimpse into the emotional progression of concussion management.

It's impossible for Earnhardt to describe the evolution of his symptoms. In a way, he said, you could say they just disappeared. One day he woke up and they were gone. But he qualifies that statement with respect to the work. He worked tirelessly, again, at Amy's urging and with her encouragement, to make damn sure those symptoms disappeared. Even when he felt fully healed and

100 percent normal, he continued to work, to make certain his senses had completely returned to baseline.

He knew the risks. And he wanted to race. It was fundamentally quite simple: He wanted to leave full-time competition on his own terms and on his own time—not when or why someone or something else made the decision for him.

He plugged right back into all those projects he'd left idle months before. He began developing Chevy's race car. He shone at corporate appearances. He sat in on meetings at JR Motorsports. He made decisions. He tried television. He liked television, and later that year he decided to make it his career.

"I feel like I'm a smarter guy, and I certainly don't take a lot of the things for granted that I did before," he said.

He certainly doesn't take Amy for granted. Half the time he won't leave her alone.

After their wedding on New Year's Eve 2016, there was a reception—and at 11 p.m. or so, the house band announced the conclusion of that celebration. Then, suddenly, the wall behind the band dropped to the floor, and there was yet another dance floor, a massive disco ball overhead, and bars in every corner. They threw a New Year's Eve party. And it was spectacular.

During the New Year's Eve bash, Lainie and I spotted Dale standing alone over near one of the bars. We hadn't seen him on his own yet, so we walked over to hug his neck and congratulate him. He had a stoic facial expression. Anyone who's gotten married can tell you the reception is a blur. You spend the entire time shaking hands and conversing with your guests. You don't spend much time with your new spouse.

Dale was looking for Amy. He told me he hadn't seen her in twenty minutes, and that twenty was entirely too damn long. Off he went. He had not yet seen her wardrobe change. Between the reception and the New Year's Eve party, Amy had changed into an evening gown, a stunning silver velvet Galvan dress that she would later wear to a spur-of-the-moment Waffle House run for some 4 a.m. smothered-'n'-covered grits. It still has syrup on it.

Amy laughed. "I've never had anybody want to be around me that much. It's just wonderful. I can't do anything around the house without him wanting to know where I am or where I'm going, and that includes going to the restroom. If I'm in the restroom, he's like, 'What are you doing in there? What's going on in there?' He's like that every day.

"It feels pretty incredible to mean that much to someone."

At that moment Junior looked up from the floor and over at her, grinned a measured trademark Earnhardt grin, curled his lip, and nodded his head.

"I don't know if anyone has ever meant this much to me," he said.

"The Middle"

In 2013, Giles High School invited its 1993 football Spartans back home to Pearisburg to acknowledge the state championship we'd won twenty years prior. The boys and I made a party of it. We drank a few beers, told old lies, and laughed until we cried about what I call Forever Friday: the brotherhood built between the lines. No matter what direction life took us individually, we became forever linked collectively by that season. (More on that in the coming pages.) They lined us up under the goalpost and announced us one by one to the crowd. Off to our right the stands were packed, loud, and rowdy. Just like the glory days. Once introduced, we trotted out to around the 30-yard line and high-fived one another. As I stood there, memories, packed away in some dormant corner of my mind, rushed back, an intoxicating cocktail that mixed Friday night butterflies and small-town big dreams with the intense pride to hang that number 9 on my back and to represent a community without even knowing it. It's a distinctive buzz, felt only by those who've played. And as I waited to hear my name from those speakers one last time, I looked around me. Standing in the end zone, in the shadow of the big red scoreboard by which we once lived and *died, the setting and the sounds were the same. The people were just as invested. The lights just as bright. But the buzz was dull. So the setting and the sounds and the lights seemed a bit duller, too. And just then it hit me: I'll never feel that exact sensation again.*

The Middle

What it was, and what it is, are one and the same...
But man, it looked different from the middle of the game...

Chapter Nine

Forever Friday

I stood in front of my house in the middle of the street, staring into the darkness, overwhelmed by the light. And I wept.

The numeral 1, comprising what looked like a million red light-bulbs positioned vertically down the center of a five-story, star-shaped steel structure high atop the Appalachian Mountain peak known as Angel's Rest, blazed brilliantly through a driving night-time snow.

My tears were the manifestation of boyhood wonder, an involuntary reaction to a dream realized, born from joy and disbelief and destiny.

To my knowledge those lights hadn't burned in thirteen years—since the last time Giles High School had won the Virginia State Football Championship. But there they shone, beacons shouting a small-town identity: We were No. 1. And that meant our community was No. 1, too.

The lights were visible from my front yard and for miles and miles beyond, well past the cattle farms and cornfields that define this region, past the stadium, Spartan Field, which just then was dormant and docile, but hours earlier had played host to a raucous celebration as we lifted rural dreams into reality.

High school football is an institution in the area of the country I'm from, ingrained in the culture of our simple-life community alongside Sunday services, potluck suppers, throwing hay, and frequent family reunions. Faith. Family. Football. That's how it is in Pearisburg.

Other sports exist, but they're recreational.

Football is an obsession from birth. In many cases it is also an expectation.

In Giles, boys begin playing organized football in the fourth grade. The Pop Warner age range spans from fourth to seventh grades, quite a discrepancy in terms of size and maturity. Bigger kids—I recall the weight tolerance being 135 pounds—were forced to warn others of their physical superiority by wearing huge black Xs, formed with electrical tape, on both sides of their helmets. But they played. The average nine-year-old boy weighs about sixty pounds. When a sixty-pound fourth grader collides with a 135-pound seventh grader, the sixty-pound fourth grader gets rocked. I was a frail little guy. I got rocked a lot, and I cried to Daddy about it.

But I was obsessed with the game. So Daddy just shrugged and told me to work harder.

In the late 1980s, there were seven Pop Warner football teams in the county, one in Rich Creek near the West Virginia border, the Lions, two in Narrows (the Lions and the Green Wave), two in Pearisburg (the Jaycees and the Lions), and two in Pembroke (the Trojans and the Spartans). When we all moved up to high school in the eighth grade, the four teams in Pearisburg and Pembroke combined to become one. There was a wealth of talent, which by the varsity level was trimmed to roughly forty kids. Since we were four years old, every last one of us had dreamed about pulling that Giles Spartan jersey, red with white numbers and white and Columbia blue stripes on the sleeves, over our shoulder pads, and to hear Mr. Harold Chafin, the public address announcer, say our names over the loudspeaker.

Some nights when I was young I sat in the press box with Mr. Chafin and my daddy, Leo. Daddy was Mr. Chafin's spotter, which meant he watched the game through binoculars to determine which player ran or caught the ball, how far he ran with it, and which defender made the tackle. He would relay that information to Mr. Chafin, who would then speak the information through the microphone to the crowd. They created their own language, reserved only for Friday nights, a sort of Southern shorthand that said a lot with a little. And they made a hell of a team, besides being next-door neighbors and close friends.

Some nights, Mr. Chafin would knock on the door of our home and ask for Daddy. He'd have a can of Old Milwaukee in each hand, and they'd sit on the couch in the den, sip a cold one, smoke some Marlboro Lights, and discuss work, life, and the Giles Spartans. I'd wander in sometimes. Daddy would promptly ask me to leave.

Daddy was so engrossed in the Spartan football mystique that he once paid for a long-distance call from Europe in order to listen to an entire game. No lie. I was probably in seventh grade or so, and he had an unexpected business trip to Germany that required a Friday night stay. So he improvised. He had me sit beside Mr. Chafin on a bench and hold the phone receiver outside the window into the night sky, so he could hear the game and feel the game and live the game. That is lunacy!

That story encapsulates the addiction. And we're not alone in Pearisburg. Those examples live in little towns all over the nation, places like Odessa, Texas, and Hoover, Alabama, and Maryville, Tennessee, and Concord, California. On and on, coast-to-coast, high school football teams are toting community dreams, dreams of young boys who yearn to someday wear the uniforms, and then the memories of old men who wore them long ago. In the glory days.

High school football is so much more than wins and losses and blocks and tackles and touchdowns. It's fathers and sons. It is a linchpin that connects families and communities, *the* marquee social event of the week and the year-round buzz in the grocery store aisle and the barbershop chair and the Pizza Hut booth. Come August, the boys strap up and slide on the pads for unbearably humid two-a-day practices, and the old men from the barbershop line the practice field for a glimpse of hope.

At its most fundamental level that's what competition is: hope.

It is then that the narrative reaches a fever pitch, which builds until the lights glow and the ball is kicked, and Spartan pride explodes in a barrage of ringing cowbells and blowing train whistles and waving bandannas.

For decades the moniker at Giles High has been the Bandana Express.

It is our battle flag.

Players are demigods; their jersey numbers and their names are painted on storefront plate-glass windows with white shoe polish, alongside the posters for Super Tuesday sale items and store hours.

Before you mock me for sounding like Buddy Garrity, the over-the-top *Friday Nights Lights* character who, even in middle age, still wears his state championship ring and takes irrational self-worth from long-gone gridiron glory, know this: The importance of high school football for those who played the game is immeasurable and it is eternal. No matter what a former player may achieve in adulthood, lessons learned between the lines are brushstrokes on the canvas of his life.

For those of us who played, Friday is every day. And Friday is forever.

I nearly quit once. It was during the break between two-a-day practices. I was leaning against a post outside the locker room, eating a peanut butter and jelly sandwich, and I said aloud that I was done with this football mess. Peter Janney, one of our toughest and most-skilled players, a running back on offense and a linebacker on defense, was leaning against a post eating his own mushy PBJ. He just laughed at me and told me to shut up and eat.

Quitting wasn't any more an option for me than it was for him.

Because quitting would have gutted our fathers. Quitting wasn't an option no matter how much bellyaching we did. I am so grateful I didn't quit.

High school football was an education in life skills. Selflessness. Accountability. Sacrifice. Work ethic. Do your job. Win gracefully and with humility. Lose gracefully without accepting mediocrity. Hate your rival as an obstacle on the field. Champion him as a man off the field. (That one comes with age.)

No matter what variables or traits separated us outside the lines, on the field we were all the same, and all pulling in the same direction toward the same goals and dreams. When we ran hills in full pads, we were all the same. Together. When we sat in the heat between practices and scarfed down those soggy sandwiches, we were the same. Together. When we wore red, white, and blue on Friday nights, we were all the same. Together. The value of that unity is difficult—maybe impossible—to understand in the moment. Time and nostalgia produce clarity about its beauty.

I've learned a common trait among many high achievers: Most hate to lose far more than they love to win. We lose far more than we win in this life. Don't sulk. Repurpose failure as fuel to learn, adjust, and improve. Those bricks were laid for me on the practice field.

From birth in Giles County, kids love Spartan football. They scrap and claw for white-and-blue minifootballs, tossed into the stands by cheerleaders at halftime, then rally their buddies to the hills surrounding the stadium to stage their own game. They idolize the players on the field, who aren't even ten years older than those kids, but they see the players as superheroes.

That's why that lit-up number 1 beaming from Angel's Rest was so radiant to me, even during a mid-December whiteout in the New River Valley. It was a commanding statement about a town fulfilled, and a defining symbol for seventeen-year-old me about the magnitude of high school football in Small Town, USA.

High school football supremacy in America is a different kind of power and a different kind of pride, regardless of the state or demographic or region. No matter what the daily grind or strife might be in a specific location, if the boys are superior on Friday night, the town is superior on Saturday morning. That is most certainly the case in Pearisburg.

Pearisburg is the county seat of Giles County. I'm long gone. But Pearisburg is who I am, and no matter where this life takes me, Pearisburg is who I will be. Small-town sensibilities, including the understanding of working for what you want and how to take care of your brother, were instilled within me there. I've taken those traits all over the world.

Giles is a rural Southern farming community. We're red, white, and blue—redneck, white liquor, and blue collar—thirty winding mountain miles off the nearest interstate, I-81. It might as well be three hundred miles. We like it that way.

Few folks who live in Pearisburg work in Pearisburg. There's not much business there, outside of farming and retail and public service. The Celanese plant in neighboring Narrows offers employment to some. Others work at the Volvo plant in Dublin. Virginia Tech, twenty miles east, is the chief employer of people in the county. Locals choose to live in Giles County and make that commute because Giles is beautiful and quaint and loyal, the heart of Appalachia and the New River Valley.

Giles is ball on Friday night and beers on Saturday night and church on Sunday morning. It's a country music song, tailgates and tan lines and hayfields. Some folks these days think that narrative is trite. Maybe it's a bit cliché, sure, but when you're from where I'm from, it is cherished and relatable.

Most folks grow up there and stay there, marry their high school sweetheart and settle down, proud to nourish the roots that their parents and their parents' parents planted generations ago. I admire them. I carry distinct guilt that I don't walk my own land often enough. But I know it is waiting, steadfast and loyal, for me to return, like Shel Silverstein's giving tree.

No other place makes me feel like my land makes me feel. Maybe it's the memories. Maybe it's the unrefined majesty of the Appalachian Mountains and the creeks and the fields. Maybe it's the isolation. The farm is nearly four hundred acres, located about fifteen miles northwest of Virginia Tech's campus. You'd swear it was fifteen hundred miles away from everything else. It is so quiet.

The water flowing in Sinking Creek is pure, easing its way to the New River. The air is crisp and light and fills your lungs. The soil is rich in nutrients to grow hay and corn and tobacco. Many of my teammates grew up working the land in Giles and hunting the deer and turkey that roamed there.

There's a barbershop, a shack called Barton's, just down the embankment from Highway 460, where dozens of flattop haircuts are given each week, the kind of Biff Tannen haircut that scalds the top of the scalp. Barton's was the chief gathering place for old men to solve the world's problems, play banjos, brag about fish they didn't catch, guzzle burnt coffee, and analyze Spartan football.

The owner, a portly ol' boy in suspenders named Clate Dollinger, would insert VHS tapes of local bluegrass concerts into the VCR, crank the knob on the Quasar TV to 11, grab a black comb to swirl up the blue Barbicide antiseptic water, fluff up the masterpiece he crafted a week ago, fire up the clippers, and go to work resculpting said masterpiece. Eight minutes later you were out the door. For the players, five of those eight minutes were spent discussing Friday night's opponent.

Mr. Clate didn't say much unless prompted. But once he got going, it was bluegrass country music school. His belly jiggled above his belt when he laughed. He had Coke-bottle glasses. And when his buddies were in there on the couches buried in old newspapers, pickin' and a-proddin', he laughed a lot. He was good to me. Back in high school his haircut fee was three dollars, and always included a hot-lather shave. I may have paid him five times in five years.

"No charge today, son. Just go beat Blacksburg," he'd say. "Good luck. We're proud of you boys."

Then he'd smile and wink and follow me outside to check on his coon dogs before tending to the next customer in line. Daddy once sat in that chair, inspired for some reason to get one of those scalp-scalding flattop cuts. Mr. Clate ran those clippers over his noggin, and Momma nearly fell out. You'd have thought she saw a ghost. She was beside-herself-pissed. Daddy just laughed.

Giles High School sits on the east side of Pearisburg, just up the hill from the New River. There's a Pizza Hut in the middle of town, and a Hardee's and a Dairy Queen over toward the west side. We didn't always pay there, either. I had my share of free Reese's Cup Blizzards. In my day those three restaurants were navigational beacons for the teenagers cruising town in their Dodge Daytonas and Chevy S-10s. We would start at the Pizza Hut, take a left on Wenonah Avenue, and drive to the stoplight at the county courthouse. Turn right on Main, past the Rite Aid pharmacy to the left and beyond the Andrew Johnson House Museum, the post office, and the Maxway Shopping Center on the right. Once past Maxway, ease catty-corner-left, past the Dairy Queen and the Tastee Freez before it went under, hook a right into Hardee's, go around the drive-thru window, and head back out again. Over and over for hours, Brooks & Dunn or Garth Brooks blaring from the

Kraco speakers you bought at Scotty's in Christiansburg, praying you got even the briefest glimpse of Jennifer or Nikole or Tessa.

The entire round-trip circuit was less than two miles. For us it was the Vegas Strip.

On fall Fridays at 4:30, Main Street, a pinched-down tributary of US Route 460, was bumper-to-bumper. The entire town was headed to the game—home or away—in a caravan of Spartan hysteria. The town lined up behind the school buses carrying the team and weaved through the mountains to the destination point. It was a hell of a spectacle.

Teachers and parents will grimace at this sentence, but classes on Fridays were useless. It was a *Peanuts* cartoon. "Wah-wah-wah…" None of us paid the teachers any mind. We'd sit there all day and go through the motions, locked in on the game plan. We wore red mesh shirts on game day, with "Spartan Football" emblazoned across the front and our jersey numbers on the back. God, we felt like titans walking through those halls. Those shirts were a status symbol, and we didn't get to keep them. They were returned after the season to ensure that no one but team members ever had them.

Those were not our game jerseys, mind you. Many schools allow players to wear their jerseys to school on game day. Not Giles High School. Our game jerseys were sacred, reserved for only Friday night.

Giles High had seven class periods each day. On fall Fridays, seventh period was reserved for the weekly schoolwide pep rally. The entire student body, faculty, and staff arrived in the gymnasium to hear our coach, Virginia High School League legend Steve Ragsdale, winner of three state championships in a Hall of Fame, thirty-year career, offer an address about the team and the opponent and the mission. Those pep rallies were intense. Our parents cut out of work early to attend, the red-and-blue Spartan mascot hand-painted on their cheeks, our jersey numbers on their backs, bandannas tied through their hair and their belt loops.

After the rally, some of my closest buddies on the team would jump in my 1985 bronze Chevy Blazer, two-door with a four-speed manual transmission. This was the one Daddy bought Momma brand-new from Mitchener Chevrolet that two weeks later had a deer stuck in the grille. Some high school boys were on their way to our farm to bail hay, and Momma let one of them drive her brand-new Blazer. He promptly struck a deer on Highway 460 and destroyed the entire front end. Seven years later Momma wanted a Ford Aerostar minivan, hunter green with tan interior, and Daddy threw me the keys to the Blazer.

So on game days the boys and I would pile in that thing after school, crank up some Guns N' Roses, and cruise Hardee's a couple of times before we headed to my house on Gale Road. I grew up one mile from Spartan Field. On Friday nights you could hear Mr. Chafin's call from our front porch. You knew when the Spartans scored a touchdown.

Mom painted the glass front door to our thousand-square-foot brick home top-to-bottom with a life-sized Spartan player wearing number 9—my number—chosen in fourth grade for two reasons: Momma's birthday was December 9, and Michael Jordan wore jersey number 9 in the 1984 Olympics. I wore it every year in every sport, unless an upperclassman claimed it first. To this day, "MS9" is stitched into the inside pocket of every suit jacket I wear on ESPN. (Buddy Garrity!)

When we walked into the house, Mom was busy mixing up a huge pot of Kraft Velveeta Shells & Cheese, economy-size, bought from the Sam's Club in Roanoke. That was our pregame meal. Every game. We were a very superstitious lot. We wore the same T-shirts under our shoulder pads for five months. This was before Kevin Plank founded Under Armour and created the moisture-wicking shirts that built his apparel empire. These were cotton tees, man, Fruit of the Loom and Hanes. By the end of the first week of practice they stood up by themselves. But we wouldn't wash them. Most of the time they were still soggy from the day before and smelled like stale sweat and teenage boys. They were disgusting.

There were five mac-'n'-cheese regulars—present, hungry, and accounted for, every week.

Raypheal Milton, our tailback, was the best pure athlete with whom I've ever competed. (The following year he would earn Virginia State Player of the Year honors, beating out future NFL star running back Thomas Jones of Powell Valley High School in the process.) Raypheal, his twin brother, Maurice—a playmaker with a gift for turning games on single plays—Jerry Saunders, and Reggie Hoston were the only four African Americans on our forty-man roster my senior season. In recent years I've wondered if they ever felt ostracized or underappreciated or disrespected—*ever*—due to race.

So I asked Raypheal, a former chef for the Carolina Panthers with whom I'm still very close, his feelings. He said that from our team, he never felt anything but brotherhood. That made me proud. And to be honest, a bit relieved.

I've always considered football to be an eraser. When the lights turn on, daily politics turn off. For a brief moment in time we're all the same. The socioeconomic, political, and racial lines that often divide us are nonexistent. We are unified as a community, all sharing the same rooting interest. It is important.

Brandon Steele, our middle linebacker, was just a sophomore. Man, he could eat. A five-foot-nine wrecking ball of a human, Brandon was the third of four boys in the Spartan Steele brothers lineage. The Steeles were clean-cut farm boys, all four born within six years of one another and raised on the land their great-granddaddy bought in 1945 for twelve hundred dollars. They lived in the original farmhouse on that land, restored by their daddy's hand in the '80s.

The Steele boys were All-State talents in a variety of sports. All of them—Stevie, Patrick, Brandon, and Micah—were handsome and popular and athletic. Patrick once teed up a golf ball in the driveway and unloaded on it. It hit me directly under my left eye; I still have the scar. Steele is a legendary name around those parts. Stevie still lives on the family land in a home he built with his own hands.

After two more trips to the state playoffs as a junior and a senior, Brandon went on to play for Joe Paterno at Penn State, alongside State College legends LaVar Arrington and Courtney Brown. He was the wedge-buster on the Nittany Lions' kickoff team and carried a 3.6 grade point average as an engineering major. JoePa loved him.

The Steele boys' mother, Vicki, was my mom's best friend. She was funny and witty and beautiful. And she didn't take any crap from those boys, either. Their daddy, Big Steve, was an intimidating figure, a godly man with callused hands and of few words. He gave me one of the worst ass-rippings I ever received. Deservedly so.

Steele Acres, the family compound in Newport, located some twenty miles from the high school, sat alongside Sinking Creek, way down a long gravel road from Virginia Route 42, which itself is a two-lane rural country highway. Once, when I was home from college, I went to pick up Stevie to throw some hay on my family farm. I tore ass down that gravel driveway, music blaring, and launched my burgundy Ford Escort off the cattle guard that separated the driveway from the path to the highway, got air, felt cool. Bad idea.

The youngest Steele, and the only girl in the family, Scarlett, was very small. And I was very young. And very stupid. Thank God Scarlett wasn't playing in the yard that day, but the point was, she could have been. And Mr. Steele let me know about it. He verbally undressed me in front of the entire family. I was mortified and defeated. And I should have been. If she had been outside, it could have been disastrous. I'll never forget the ire in his eyes that day. I'd disappointed him. He expected more of me than that. And he should've.

Brian Cumbee and David Greever, a pair of offensive linemen, were there every week. Like me, Cumbee and Greever were over-achievers, all heart and desire. Glue guys. That's one reason we got along. Overachievers were the norm for our team. We had some really good players, but other than Raypheal, no real superstars. We were a collection of young men with precise goals and a keen understanding of expectation, rare personality cohesion, excellent leadership, and great coaching.

And none of us were afraid to dream. We *expected* to win.

I was our left cornerback and punt returner. To this day, I main-tain that I was the least-talented starting player in my high school's distinguished football history. In a lot of ways I was a liability on the field. I knew that then and I know that now. I was plenty athletic, but I wasn't fast and I wasn't strong. I got run clean over multiple times trying to fill a hole and stop an opponent, a speed bump for oppos-ing runners on the road to the end zone. Much like in Pop Warner, the weight difference didn't add up. When the equation is 140 sta-tionary pounds versus 170 pounds in motion, it rarely ends well.

But nobody wanted it worse than me. Nobody worked harder. Nobody dreamed bigger. In football, I wasn't blessed with the ability to beat most of my teammates or opponents with God-given skill. If I wanted the opportunity to play, I had to outwork others. Daddy stressed desire to me all day, every day. He called it "want-to." I just wanted to make him proud, and nothing ever made him prouder than what my teammates and I achieved in the fall of 1993, when we reignited the lights.

Last, nobody had more passion than I did for the entire Fri-day night equation, which held many variables: The smell when sweat mixes with cheap laundry detergent and Windex and sticker glue. The brightness difference between our practice pants and our game pants. The small rips and the permanent white scuffs on the shoulders of our red home jerseys, left over from previous hits on previous Friday nights. The *click-clack* cadence of the school-issued screw-in cleats walking the concrete hallway that separated the locker room from the agriculture building, in which we convened to sit in the dark and the quiet, and let the juxtaposition between the stillness around us and the adrenaline within us bubble.

The single-file walk from the ag building to the field, through a tunnel of townsfolk screaming our names, always looking for Momma, to the foot of the near goalpost, welded in a long-ago GHS shop class, shaped like an H, not a Y. The smell of boiling nuclear-pink hot dogs bathed in chili and wrapped in aluminum foil—Daddy called them devil dogs and ate five a week. The thundering echo of a hundred hands slapping thigh pads in unison, crashing through the musical symphony from the Marching Spartans, under the direction of my dear friend Rick Sparks. The smell of grass beneath our feet during pregame calisthenics, cut earlier that morning by my position coach, Jeff Williams.

Coach Williams was a GHS defensive back in the mid-'80s, and he lived for Spartan football, one of those überintense movie characters that every school has on its staff, wearing nut-hugger Bike coaching shorts and a tucked-in T-shirt, rolled-down white tube socks, and black Spot-Bilt cleats with white shoestrings. I swore he wore that whistle around his neck to bed, blew it in his sleep. He would eventually take over as head coach and win a state championship of his own. His enthusiasm was infectious and impactful, but damn—every one of us under his watch wanted to punch him in the face. He never stopped yapping at us. He once said something to me that resonates even still.

I was the holder for the field goal unit, and Maurice Milton, Raypheal's twin brother whom I mentioned earlier, was the kicker. We were practicing extra points one evening, and I lamented out loud how badly I wanted to get the hell out of practice.

That comment pissed Coach Williams off. "Don't say that.

Dammit. Don't. Say. That," he repeated, honest to God on the brink of tears. "These are the days, boys. These are the best days of your lives. You will never get these days back, and you will miss them so much. You'll miss your teammates. You'll miss the fans. You'll even miss practice and me riding your ass. Trust me on this. I'd give *anything* to go back. I'd cut my leg off to put those pads on one more time. So don't wish it away."

You know what? He was right. That was the unequivocal truth. Every one of us misses that specific feeling of camaraderie and belonging. Every one of us would love to run onto that field with those friends and those smells and those sounds and that expectation and that adulation once again. Any time we're together as adults, that's the conversation. Because nothing else offers that exact emotion.

And the lights—the towering lights. The way they burst over the crowd and bounced off the helmets. The way the entire scene looked through the red face mask on my own helmet. The down-ups and the jumping jacks and the barking cadence of Swing 44, our signature off-tackle running play.

Down! Two!...Ready Set...Hut!

Pageantry and tradition are intoxicating. There was a gentleman named Arnold Tickle, the captain of the signature Spartan train whistle, clad for some reason in Columbia blue Bike coaching shorts and matching "Single Wingin'" T-shirt, who would scamper down out of the bleachers to the track when our games were well in-hand. Once in position, he would turn to the crowd, begin furiously waving his bandanna flag, and yell:

DOWN BY THE RIVER!

At which time the packed bleachers would echo: DOWN BY THE RIVER!

WE TOOK A LITTLE WALK!

(WE TOOK A LITTLE WALK!)

WE MET UP WITH THE GREEN WAVE!
(WE MET UP WITH THE GREEN WAVE!)
AND WE HAD A LITTLE TALK!
(AND WE HAD A LITTLE TALK!)
WE KICKED 'EM IN THE RIVER!
(WE KICKED 'EM IN THE RIVER!)
AND WE HUNG 'EM ON THE LINE!
(AND WE HUNG 'EM ON THE LINE!)
WE CAN BEAT THE GREEN WAVE!
(WE CAN BEAT THE GREEN WAVE!)
ANY DAMN TIME!
(ANY DAMN TIME!)

And the entire assemblage would erupt in cheers. That chant was the stamp on victory, and it remains a decades-old Giles Spartans tradition.

Again, it's not just us. It's a microcosm of the high school football thread that weaves through the American fabric. Everyone knows the title of H. G. Bissinger's timeless book, *Friday Night Lights*. What they may not know is the book's telling subtitle: *A Town, a Team, and a Dream.*

That's it. Right there. High school football provides an outlet for countless little Nowhere, America, towns, just like Pearisburg, to feel that they're a part of something bigger. It gives them a license to dream when other parts of their lives may not.

And in the fall of 1993, we were the cord in the outlet that once again fed power to the lights.

That's why I stood in the middle of the street in front of my house, in tears.

Because atop a mountain where there was often darkness, we had created light.

Chapter Ten

Sam, You There?

Most days the mother would park at the entrance gate of the Navy golf course in San Diego and unload her son. The boy was not quite ten years old, and that meant he wasn't of age to play a round. So he'd hop from the car, wave good-bye to his mom, and then snake along the south side of the ditch line that separated the clubhouse parking lot from the first and second fairways.

His path was strategic. The clubhouse and its rules police couldn't see the south side.

The boy would gather sticks and grass and branches and leaves along the way. And when he was certain they could no longer see him, he would lie down in the ditch and bury himself in the natural camouflage. And he would wait.

Eventually, inevitably, the father would arrive at the boy's position. And every time the father would pose the same question to the breeze: "Sam, you there?"

Sam was there. Of course he was there, bursting just then with the rush of the father's beckoning. And Sam would pop up from the ditch and brush off the debris and run into his father's embrace. Then they would climb in a golf cart and off they'd go, father and son, together.

And Earl and Sam Woods would play golf until the sun gave way to the stars and they could no longer see the ball. And it was during those rounds that Earl's boy, Sam—Eldrick Tont Woods—became Tiger.

"I don't know why he called me Sam," Woods said through his signature sheepish grin on a brilliant morning in March 2018. He looked directly at me when he said it. *That* stare. Penetrating. Then he looked through me. Then beyond me, that iconic toothy smile now running from his lips. "I asked him [why] when he was still alive, and he says, 'I don't know, you look like a Sam to me.' So my nickname—beyond my [other] nickname—is Sam."

Maybe that's common knowledge to hard-core golf fans. But I'd never heard it before. So in that moment I felt connected to Tiger. He actually seemed slightly vulnerable. Before this, I'd seen Woods only on television, and I'd never seen him unguarded. Just then, to me at least, his demeanor felt disarmed and reflective, reborn almost. That comes with humility. And Tiger Woods, admittedly, during this interview, was a humbled man.

Countless books, articles, and programs have been devoted to Woods's life and career, written or produced by former coaches or golf journalists who have covered him professionally and known him personally. Some of those passages detail Woods's failed marriage and former mistresses, famous girlfriends, or his obsessive Navy SEAL training.

I did not take that route. We've seen his low points plenty. I wanted a vulnerable peek at the rebirth. Because I believe in redemption and am inspired by redemption. And I wondered what his perspective was on this new life. I had the blessing to ask some questions I'd always wondered about him, and that my dad had wondered about him. My dad loved Woods's competitive ferocity, and throughout the years between Tiger's PGA Tour debut and my father's death in 2008, Dad and I had many memorable discussions while watching Woods fist-pump his way toward Masters lore. It was every golf fan's dream: to sit a spell with this captivating figure and talk life.

Woods was very gracious to me. He agreed to a twenty-minute chat. He wound up sitting with us for thirty.

The most memorable moment might have been before the interview, during the initial meeting. I sat inside the clubhouse at Woods's home course, the Medalist Golf Club, in Hobe Sound, Florida, chugging Starbucks and preparing final notes for our interview. I wasn't nervous, but I sure as hell wasn't relaxed, either.

As I stared at my notes, a shadow washed across the doorway to my left. I looked up. It was Woods. And Larry Fitzgerald, the all-world NFL wide receiver. I didn't rightly know how to react. I stood up, and Woods walked over and said hello. We shook hands and he said the funniest, most disarming thing:

"You know what was amazing, and hilarious? When you chugged that beer with Dale Earnhardt Jr. after his last NASCAR race! One of the best things I've seen on ESPN!"

I can't lie. That amped me up. Supercharged me. I didn't need that coffee anymore. His comment infused me with confidence. I told him right then to go win the Masters and we'd do the same thing—that I'd be waiting on him at the 18th green with a couple of those fabled three-dollar drafts from the concession stand.

For the interview, he sat directly across from me on a black director's chair, just outside the clubhouse at Medalist, overlooking the course. It was a humid Florida morning in March. We sat close together, our knees maybe a foot apart. In real life that's too close. But TV cameras always require a reduction of personal space.

I learned so much in that half hour, including the role those rounds with his father at the Navy course played in shaping Sam into one of the greatest golfers who ever lived, a prodigy realized. Father and son spent afternoons on the old back nine, the run-down backside of the course's original 18 holes, hidden off in the corner, hitting balls for hours. No words; ball striking club the lone sound made. With time, the rounds became the competitive foundation for a first-name legacy.

Tiger.

"It was nothing but focus," he said, the smile racing back now. "Because we knew at the end of the week, the true litmus test is going to be Saturday and Sunday, who was going to beat who. And he has to get ready to beat his little son. And I was getting ready to kick my dad's butt. And we would sit there and practice and practice and practice. That was fun, I thoroughly miss it."

Woods was once the most dominant competitive force in sports. He was part magician, part assassin. He believes the best golf shot of his life was in 2002, at Hazeltine Golf Club in Minnesota. He remembered the club (3-iron) and the location (18th bunker from the fairway). Athletes remember. Especially golfers. That memory can be a detriment for Woods. He putts on memory, and golf courses reshape greens, modernize them, and reposition holes.

"I remember certain putts breaking a certain way," he said. "I can tell you the year. I could tell you the round. I can tell you how hard, what I did with it, where I missed it, where I made it. I can tell you all that. But when they put down new greens, I putt with memory, and sometimes the putts just don't break that way anymore. It will get to me."

His competitiveness is legendary. I learned its evolution that day. Woods's original goal was simple: to earn a tour card. He laughed when he said it because, his résumé now historic, it sounds ridiculous coming from his mouth. He just wanted to make a living. He just wanted an opportunity to play golf.

"I didn't have what I have now," he said. "Winning felt differently, because I was able to prove myself against these top players in the world. I was able to [become] the number one player in the world. I was able to win Majors. I was able to win consistently for a long period of time. And the evolution of how it feels to win hasn't changed the gratification that I feel when it's done.

"But I'd have to say, the process I went through has changed, because I've gone through different swings. I've gone through different injuries. But ultimately, if I'm holding the trophy, no one else is."

I wondered what made him so unstoppable for so long. I wasn't prepared for his blunt answer.

"I just wanted to beat you."

"It can't be that simple, man. It just can't."

"It really is. It really is."

"How?"

"When I compete...," he began, and paused before continuing, "I get immersed into the competition of it. And I just love—not just to win—I love to beat people."

What a comment. That's the assassin talking.

"And I love to go head-on, *at somebody*, eyeball to eyeball; let's see who flinches first. I thoroughly enjoy that part of it."

He paused. I listened.

"And that has kept me going, I think, on weeks where other tour players say they're tired, won a couple tournaments back-to-back, and they're not really into it. If I'm teed up, my whole goal is to beat you. That's it. I have always loved that aspect of it."

My mind said, *Whoa! Hell yeah!* My mouth said nothing.

"Has it driven me, sometimes, too far? Yeah, it has. I've caused myself some bodily harm because of it. I have pushed my body beyond its limits, and that's where I am, for the past few years, why I've hurt my knee. I've gone through so much to try and beat you. Unfortunately, I wish I had a little more of a governor. I could've not put myself in these situations."

He paused. I just kept listening. Didn't say a word.

"But on the flip side of it, I don't think I would have won by the margins I've been able to win by. They would have been a bit closer."

In recent years, PGA Tour dominance had seemed a bygone pursuit. This once-unstoppable, impermeable force was broken. And so here he was, forty years old and unable to get up out of bed by himself. For six months, he needed assistance to stand. In that period, two things drove him: his kids and the pain.

His dreams no longer included historic performances or iconic trophies or jackets or legacies. He did not obsess about driving golf balls to nuclear distances or putting them with a surgeon's precision. Those thoughts were the furthest from his mind. Yes, it was that talent, coupled with an assassin's conscience, that made him the most famous athlete on the planet. But that talent also created an obsession to dominate opponents. The constant grind to reach new competitive heights, and the unyielding search for new methods to reach those heights, had finally caught him.

His prayer was to eliminate the debilitating back pain that had consumed his life and just be Daddy, tap a soccer ball around the yard with his daughter, Sam, or lie on the floor and snap some Legos together with his son, Charlie. This most complex man wanted simple moments that eluded him because his back was so painful.

"It was really disheartening," he said. "I tried to suck it up as much as I possibly could, but then there were times where I just couldn't get up from where I was."

We all fall. It is human to fall and to fail. It is also human to find inspiration in a good comeback story. And there's no comeback story quite like that of Tiger Woods. Before the deafening roars, and the prodigious climb, and the legendary performances, and the crashing fall, and the resurgent ascension, he was much like the rest of us, a hardheaded teen. The consummate example is his traditional Sunday red golf shirt.

"It goes back to my mom," he said. "My mom says that my power color is red. And so, in junior golf I won a golf tournament wearing red, and she said, 'See, I told you, red.' So, the very next tournament what did I do? I wore blue. I win again. I told her, and I just kind of made fun of it, poked at her a little bit, and I think I lost the next two out of three tournaments wearing blue. Switched to red and I went on a hot streak. And, well...I kept it."

Lesson: Always listen to Momma.

He figured he peaked in 1987, at eleven years old. He entered thirty-six tournaments that year and won them all. He also aced sixth grade, straight As all year. And he practiced, neurotically, with an attention to detail well beyond his years and a mischievous edge that suggested his youth.

"I would just drive my mom crazy when I used to put her crystal up on a table, and I used to hit flop shots over it," he said, laughing. "Now, that's real pressure, by the way."

Woods told me he figured he left twelve Major championships on the table. I asked for clarification. Twelve wins? No. Twelve opportunities to win. He explained that Augusta National Golf Club plays well for him. He likes the sight lines and loves to putt on those glassy greens that four times had resulted in his winning the green jacket.

"There's no better feeling than going into that back nine with a chance to win, and you know it—and everyone else knows it," he said, still smiling that smile. "And to hear the roars—and you know who the roars are for. You know where the groups are located. That's an Ernie [Els] roar. And that's definitely a Phil [Mickelson] roar, up there. You just know how people cheer for certain people. You can get a sense of that, and it's really neat."

He vividly recalled the first Masters victory experience, starting with the green jacket. It was huge. And warm.

"I was swimming in it. It's iconic memorabilia, and I was

wearing it, something I saw all the greatest champions that I've ever seen, growing up, they all won it," he said. "And here I am at twenty-one years old wearing a green jacket. That night I tipped back, probably, too many. Actually, I know it was too many.

"And I end up going to sleep with it as my blanket. I cuddled up next to it and I was holding it like a little blankie. That's how much it meant to me to win the Masters. And to do it with my dad still alive... That was awesome."

Like many athletes and celebrities in the twilights of notable careers, Woods wants to change the world with philanthropy. His vision? Empowering children through education. On September 11, 2001, Woods was in St. Louis, Missouri. Two days later, with planes grounded nationwide, he drove home to Florida. It was during that drive he realized life's fragility and the importance of paying blessings forward.

"If I was one of the casualties, no one would have really cared about my golf," he said. "What was the leave-behind? There was really nothing. Hitting golf balls? It's not a leave-behind."

The TGR Foundation is his leave-behind. TGR uses a science, technology, engineering, and math (STEM) curriculum to help prepare sixth through twelfth graders for college educations and professional careers. Woods said TGR is improving opportunities for millions of kids around the globe.

"You know, I [golf] for my own selfish desires," he explained. "To compete, to play, to satisfy this urge to beat people. But at the end of the day it's about, what are you going to leave behind for the next generation? How can you leave the world you came into a better place? Well, that's very simple for me—that's my foundation."

Well after this interview, in the 2018 PGA Tour finale at East Lake Golf Club in Atlanta, Woods won again. He had learned to play golf in a way completely different from the way he used to dominate the sport for so many years. His spine was fused, so he didn't have the same range of motion and thus couldn't create the same angles with his swing. He had the power; he just had to learn to handle new limitations.

But the pain was gone.

He explained it to me this way: It was like riding a bike, but a new bike. And that led to a new life. And now he's continuing to work and learn how to live that new life.

As we parted ways, I kept thinking how learning to live with new limitations applies to all of us in one part of our lives or another.

REDEMPTION

The eighteenth green at Augusta National Golf Club was an adoring throng, the likes of which the age-old game had rarely seen, thousands of onlookers awestruck by the scene they witnessed, keenly aware of its uniquely historic position at this uniquely historic place.

Winning the Masters Tournament is a life-altering accomplishment for any man, the ultimate peak in every golfer's climb. Winning it for the fifth time is a timeless image. Just two men have done so.

Winning it two years removed from barely being able to get out of bed and walk is a miracle. Just one man has done so.

That man is Tiger Woods.

And on the day he did it, April 14, 2019, as Woods strode uphill, up the famed eighteenth fairway at Augusta, toward the clubhouse and toward a coronation, the massive assemblage was reverent and appreciative. And as he rolled the final putt toward the bottom of the cup to culminate what may be the greatest comeback story in sports history, Masters patrons cheered his name like no man had ever been cheered here.

TI-GER! TI-GER! TI-GER!

At Augusta National, there is no digital scoreboard. The

scoreboards are manual, updated by human hands placing numbered placards within the billboard facings of stationary towers.
Even the men responsible for placing and replacing those placards
cheered. Stood and cheered. Stood and cheered and clapped and
beamed.

It was raucous in a way Augusta is never raucous.

And as that putt fell into the annals of Masters legend, Woods
turned to see his son, Charlie, sprinting into his arms, and joy
blanketed the scene like pollen, most faces incapable of stifling
a smile. Some grinned through tears. In that moment, many of
us were whisked immediately back to 1997, when Tiger, then just
twenty-one, barely a man himself, marched into his own father's
arms in the same spot, standing atop the mountain, father and
son, pupil and student, for the very first time.

Later that evening Woods recalled that moment, and defined
for us the true sweetness of the moment with Charlie on the fringe
of the eighteenth, informing us that during the 83rd Masters
Tournament, his kids, daughter Sam and son Charlie, got to see
golf bring their father happiness unlike any they'd seen before.

Before then, Tiger stated, they had only seen the game bring
him pain and frustration.

And after he hugged his children and his mother, he hugged
his agent, Mark Steinberg, and his publicist, Glenn Greenspan,
the folks who stood behind him when he, himself, could not
stand and when so many turned away. And he walked through
a tunnel of patrons, ten rows deep and rowdy, snaking from the
eighteenth green to the scoring station, a distance of maybe one
hundred yards, through this receiving line of sorts, at the end of
which stood a group of past Masters champions that included
Zach Johnson and Bernhard Langer and Adam Scott and Bubba
Watson, and extended into a gaggle of the brightest young stars in
the game today, from Justin Thomas to Rickie Fowler to Brooks

Koepka to Xander Schauffele, most of whom idolized Woods as boys, waiting like eager fans for high fives and hugs, every bit as awestruck as we were, and far more aware of just how miraculous it was that they actually just saw what they *actually just saw.*

We all knew we were both witnessing history and were somehow a small part of it. The air felt humble, both at seeing excellence restored and by the reminder that redemption is beautiful.

We will tell our grandchildren we were there.

And I will tell mine that as I stood there taking in the moment, scribbling feverishly within the pages of a leather-bound notepad the details of the scene in which I was enveloped, two gentlemen approached me. They were campus ministers at Clemson University. And one of them said the most profound thing.

They said they saw themselves in Woods's triumphant, transcendent moment.

I asked why.

"Because we're all capable of big mistakes. But we all have the opportunity for redemption, too."

You'ns

Legendary NCAA basketball coach Bob Huggins (Huggy Bear) had a cup of coffee in the NBA, a brief stint with the Philadelphia 76ers. At the time, Philly's roster was loaded with future Hall of Fame players, including one of the greatest ever, Julius Erving. Huggy Bear didn't last too long. This man is a world-class basketball coach— and a world-class storyteller, as evidenced by this description of his time with the Sixers on the Marty Smith's America *podcast:*

It's a very cold business. Three of us got cut—the first-round pick, the second-round pick, and me. The trainer came in and he said, "You'ns wanna know who made it, or who didn't make it?" That's what they say over there in Philadelphia, "you'ns." Those two guys jumped up and said, "Just tell us who made it, man!" And he said, "None of you [expletives]." And he ran out the door. He was a jokester, so those two guys thought he was joking. So they wait a couple minutes and he doesn't come back. So they're running up and down the halls trying to find him. Me? I'm grabbing all the gear I can find to take home for mementos. You got to be smart enough to know when you're not good enough. And I wasn't good enough. I shot the ball really well. But I'm there with World B. Free, with Doug Collins, with Julius Erving, with Harvey Catchings, Darryl Dawkins. I was in awe. The things they do, you're just standing there with your mouth open in amazement, just to be that close to see the things those guys can do. Absolutely incredible. I mean, come on. I knew there wasn't any need for me there. I don't know why they kept me as long as they did. But I'm glad they did. Because otherwise I might have been doing something else other than coaching right now.

Chapter Eleven

Gifted

Unconditional love is the rare fortress built not from steel but from selflessness. Impenetrably vulnerable, its meekness is its strength, its transparency its shield. It knows no boundaries or definitions or qualifications.

It just...is...a language universally translated through compassion.

To give unconditional love, most of us must be stripped of a certain pride, which develops as a defense mechanism, and then be rebuilt from a new foundation of humility. At least that was what I had to do. It took a while. Others possess it naturally and share it readily, with no effort.

Lizzie Delle Donne is one of those people.

The oldest of Ernie and Joanie Delle Donne's three children, Lizzie was born deaf and blind, and she suffers from autism and cerebral palsy. She is nonverbal, but that's not to say she can't speak. She has plenty to say.

From the time they were toddlers, Lizzie's siblings knew her unconditional love, and, more importantly, they knew it was the mission of their lives to ensure she felt their love.

"A lot was innate," explains Lizzie's younger sister, Elena. "My parents never really had to say anything. Every time I think of Lizzie, I get that touching feeling, that emotion. She's an angel. And somehow our family was blessed enough to get her. From day one, she's been the superstar of the family."

In the Delle Donne family, that is no small statement. As a high school senior, Elena and Lizzie's brother, Gene, was the top-rated quarterback in Delaware, and he went on to play Division I college football at Duke University and then Middle Tennessee State.

Elena, though, is on another level. Elena is an Olympic gold medalist, among the best women's basketball players in the world and among the most recognizable athletes in America.

Basketball is her image. Family is her identity. Especially Lizzie.

In high school, Elena was the most prolific female player in the country. Every university courted her, including one of the most dominant dynasties in the history of sports: the University of Connecticut women's basketball program, led by legendary head coach Geno Auriemma.

Elena chose to attend UConn. In the weeks and months leading up to college, she shielded herself from even considering the emotional prospect of being so far away from Lizzie.

She made it two days in Storrs.

Ten years later, even still, discussing the moment moves her to tears.

"Eighteen years old, I was leaving for Connecticut, and I still remember to this day saying good-bye to Lizzie," Elena says, eyes welling, voice cracking a bit. "It makes me sad talking about it. I got on my knees and I just hugged her, and buried my head in my big sister's chest. I just couldn't do it."

At that moment, Elena's priority scale became clear: She loved basketball. But she loved Lizzie more. So she left UConn and transferred closer to home, to the University of Delaware.

"There's so much more—all eighteen years of my life [prior] she taught me that, and I realized it was time to come home," Elena continues. "And my goodness was it the right decision. My life is Lizzie. She'll always have a huge impact in my life. I needed to be close to her."

There were moments—especially when Elena and Gene were young—that produced lasting lessons. Initially they were unaware that Lizzie was any different, because Ernie and Joanie treated Lizzie just the same as the other two kids. But with age come knowledge and judgment, and the inevitable ebb of innocence.

When Elena was in kindergarten, she invited a classmate over to her home and introduced her to Lizzie. Immediately and hysterically, the friend began to cry, telling Elena she wanted to leave.

"She called Lizzie a monster," Elena says, again emotional. "That was the first time where I was like, 'Wow, she must be different to what other people see.' I didn't realize she was that different."

In that moment, an impossible hurt for a parent, Joanie chose not to judge, but rather to teach.

"My mom probably was feeling anger at the time with how my friend reacted," Elena says. "But she was able to explain, 'Yeah, Lizzie is different, but look at all the other gifts she has, and look at all the things she brings to this family.'

"And also, 'Look at how your friend reacted. There's not enough instances where she's interacted with someone who has special needs.' So right away, I knew I needed to get Lizzie out there more, and have people see her. That is very important to me."

In moments like that Elena learned selflessness from her mother. Joanie refuses to let anyone feel bad for her, or even to acknowledge the challenge of caring for Lizzie, which Elena says is often like caring for a newborn.

On a normal day, Joanie wakes Lizzie and gets her up, dresses her, and feeds her breakfast. Weekdays, from 9 a.m. to 3 p.m.,

Lizzie attends the Mary Campbell Center, where she participates in various activities with residents. Some days she'll swim; some days she'll hang in a beanbag chair that vibrates to the beat of the music it plays. This is how she experiences the outside world.

At 3 p.m., she comes home and eats, maybe a cheese stick and some Cheerios. Then it's dinner, bath, and some couch time. Lizzie enjoys sitting and tumbling and balancing.

"It's interesting to watch how athletic she is on that couch," Elena says. "I couldn't do any of that stuff."

There were countless moments throughout the years when well-laid plans were abruptly dashed as Ernie and Joanie rushed Lizzie to the hospital. Like Thanksgiving 1997, when they sped out the door, Lizzie in the midst of a seizure, turkey in the oven. Gotta go.

Elena was eight. Gene was eleven. Neither knew how to cook. So they turned off the oven and bummed a ride from a family friend to Boston Market.

"Lizzie, by far, has had the biggest impact on my worldview, even from childhood," Elena says. "Little kids are so egocentric, me, me, me. From day one it was her. My whole life I've grown up with that perspective, that other people need so much more than what I need.

"That's made me a lot more selfless and giving, and able to pick up on what people are feeling or needing. They don't always have to speak it for me to be able to feel it and understand it, because I've had to figure Lizzie out my entire life."

When I met Elena and Lizzie they were on a red golf cart together, cruising down the lengthy gray driveway at the family compound just outside Wilmington, Delaware, Elena at the wheel.

This is one of Lizzie's most treasured activities, little sister's arm around her back, wind in her face.

The oaks lining the drive are meaty and commanding, stately, tall enough to crane the neck, a natural canopy placed there by the

DuPont family more than a century ago. Yes, *that* DuPont family, the same surname that adorned the hood of Jeff Gordon's race car for twenty years and that hangs over the doors of countless Delaware elementary and secondary schools.

These thirty acres provided their summer refuge. These days the property offers privacy and comfort to another influential Delaware bunch—the Delle Donne family. Fall has dawned over the Northeast, but the air is unseasonably warm. The foliage is orange and yellow and red and vibrant and sun-drenched. It is a beautiful scene.

I wondered aloud how the family knows that Lizzie knows who they are. Truth is, Elena says, there's no indisputable way to prove it. But watching the sisters interact makes it rather obvious. Lizzie embraces Elena and she giggles, so she knows.

Since Lizzie can neither see nor hear, her senses of smell and touch are heightened. A relationship with her is based on proximity, physical closeness. She and Elena must be next to each other, touching. The tangibility requirement within their relationship is even represented on Elena's signature Nike basketball shoes. On the back of each tongue is a pink, raised, tactile rendering of the tattoo on Elena's side—Lizzie's name with angel's wings.

Lizzie must be able to smell another's scent, feel the unique characteristics of his or her skin. One of the first things Lizzie does when encountering someone is grab their head and pull it close to her nose for a sniff.

The smell of shampoo is interesting to her.

I asked Elena if she'd used the same shampoo for twenty-five years. She has not. But she has always put Moroccan oil in her hair to maintain consistency. Joanie, meanwhile, has worn the same perfume—Chanel—for Lizzie's entire life. Lizzie's sense of smell is so acute that Elena believes she can likely distinguish individuals based on the smell of their unique combination of skin oils.

"She tells us a lot about perspective, and never getting too self-consumed, and realizing there's so much more out there and so many more people you can impact, can make a difference in their lives," Elena says.

"Lizzie has achieved so much more in life than I'll ever achieve on the basketball floor. It's pretty nice that I get to put a ball through a basketball hoop and have a huge stadium of people cheering for me while I'm doing that.

"Lizzie gets a diagnosis when she's born, saying you'll never walk a day in your life, you'll never be able to lift your head. And she's done all that, and more, without a crowd watching her and cheering her on. That's special."

And so that's the story of the Delaware Delle Donnes. Lizzie first. Always. No matter what. Unconditionally.

Sometimes that means surrendering the steak on your plate so Lizzie can have two steaks. Sometimes that means rocking her on the couch. Sometimes that means a trip to the hospital. Sometimes that means a golf cart ride around the property.

"She takes my steak. A lot," Elena says with a laugh. "I started telling my mom to get her two steaks, so we can all eat, too."

Chapter Twelve

Father Time

Time is the rarest resource. While the drop of rain and the morsel of food cycle through its prism—returning again and again in alternate forms—time itself cannot be manufactured, re-created, retained, or corralled.

The clock's every tick is a moment then a memory.

Time is relentless, which we cannot grasp in the moment. Granted, we try. But we cannot. Because it's not until we stumble upon context—our oldest child's baby picture deep in a closet, or a gray hair staring us down in the mirror—that we truly consider time's passage.

And as long days give way to short years, the memories of our moments flicker in a filmstrip of snapshots, providing an emotional bridge from what is to what was.

No matter how much time we have, we always want more.

I was reminded of this on a humid November day in 2015. The air in west Alabama was sticky and still, muggier even than normal for a fall morning in Tuscaloosa, so thick you'd swear you were watching microscopic droplets of moisture bounce through the beams of the sunrise, just as microscopic beads of sweat formed on your brow.

It was like being in a bathroom with the hot shower cranked.

I was standing in Nick Saban's driveway, just outside his garage. The door was open, and his black Mercedes sat patiently while my crew crawled around its tan interior, installing a pair of GoPro cameras in the upper corners of its crystal clear windshield and stationing a sound pack in its backseat.

That may be the only time anyone ever touched that backseat.

The boys worked with great efficiency, considering every moment with care and respect for Saban's time. Saban doesn't do inefficient. So anyone hoping for his time better not do inefficient, either.

I was concerned about even crossing the threshold into the garage, and thereby crossing the threshold of his privacy. I'd never met the man. (Most folks around these parts would write that sentence differently, like this: I'd never met *The Man*.) I had no concept of what to expect, and I didn't feel comfortable assuming I was welcome in his space.

It was a Wednesday, sometime around 7 a.m. CT.

And it was LSU Week.

Les Miles's Tigers were unbeaten and second-ranked among college football teams in America. Saban's Tide were ranked fourth, having lost just once, in week 3 to the Ole Miss Rebels. If Alabama lost to LSU four days from now, any shot at a Southeastern Conference Championship—let alone a National Championship—would be over.

Saban had a lot on his mind.

He lives some fifteen minutes from the University of Alabama campus, where the college football empire he's built is considered by some as history's greatest, better even than the only man in the debate with him—and from the same school, no less—Bear Bryant.

To Bama fans, Nick Saban is a god. He extracted them from years of college football exile and marched them toward a certain promised land. And like Bryant before him, he is most certainly worshipped.

Make no mistake: Alabama football is religion.

On the ride into town that morning I noticed the line at the Waffle House. It was out the door, winding past the plate-glass windows boasting "Roll Tide" in crimson and white script with the school's mascot, Al the Elephant, peering on.

That struck me: Nick Saban's football team is the heart of this town—and at least half of the state—pumping life to the furthest tips of its appendages. I already knew that. But until I saw it first-hand, I didn't *know*.

To folks Saban doesn't know and doesn't yet trust, he can be intimidating. Abrasive. Anybody who tells you different is lying. He doesn't suffer BS. Ask anyone who's ever worked for him.

You're either great or you're gone.

But conversely, he respects fully and engages completely in prepa-ration and thoughtfulness. If you show up prepared and passion-ate, he'll reciprocate. That trait is nearly universal. Fundamentally, it's the Golden Rule: Treat me in the way you want to be treated.

I didn't yet know all of this about Saban when he emerged from the side door of his home and said hello. But I did feel pre-pared for what was about to happen.

He asked what we were doing, even though he already knew. Saban knows. He was told we'd hop in the Benz and ride to the football office at the Mal Moore Athletic Complex on the Ala-bama campus, chat along the way, and make some television.

We got in the car. Just Saban and me.

I felt like I was in the car with my new girlfriend's dad or some-thing, not exactly sure what to say to this guy I'd just met and des-perately wanted to impress—and who more than likely felt that I was encroaching on his territory. That would have been a fair emotion.

The goal was to produce a self-contained five-minute inter-view, which would require no editing and roll directly on-air, as is, on ESPN's *SportsCenter* program.

One shot, kid.

My philosophy toward initial meetings with interview subjects is to take a fan's perspective—ask what interests me. It's a thirty-thousand-foot view, not insider depth.

At the time, when I thought *Saban*, I thought *the Process*. Well, what the hell was the Process? I wanted to find out, from the source. But first, I wondered aloud how many times a day he heard the Bama battle cry: "Roll Tide."

I mentioned to him that I'd seen it on that Waffle House win-dow. That was my icebreaker with the new girlfriend's dad: "Hey man, honored to meet you. I saw the Waffle House had Roll Tide painted on the windows. How many times a day do you hear that?"

Hell of a first impression.

For whatever reason—probably pity at just how stupid the ques-tion was—it worked. He laughed. So I laughed. From there, we just chatted. My second question was about the Process. He explained—and this is paraphrased—that it's the emotional and physical devel-opment of each individual player to become the most prepared, most accountable version of himself, so that the man beside him might become the most prepared, most accountable version of *himself*, and that man by man, individual by individual, the evo-lution toward personal excellence becomes a movement toward an unyielding standard of team excellence.

Outwork yesterday.

The Process is another fundamental life lesson: The greatest in any field are almost always those willing to be coached—in other words, those always willing to accept guidance in the effort to improve. The greatest lead by example. The weakest follow the greatest—and they either adapt or they get gone.

The final topic I wondered about was focus. Saban's is legendary. While preparing to meet him, I'd read an article about his agent, Jimmy Sexton, in which Sexton described Saban's focus.

He said if Saban was driving down the street and a bomb went off, and no shrapnel hit his car, Saban wouldn't know the bomb went off because he's so laser-focused on football.

I told Saban that exact story, and I asked how he would describe his focus level.

He laughed again. Big ol' grin. I wasn't sure if I should laugh this time.

He told me a story.

When he was the defensive coordinator at Michigan State many moons ago—this was in the mid-1980s—he was out recruiting in Youngstown, Ohio, and had lunch with legendary high school coach Bob Stoops. This was Uncle Bob Stoops, not his nephew Bob—the former University of Oklahoma head coach who led the Sooners to the 2000 National Championship.

So Saban and Uncle Bob were in a bar, eating and tossing back a couple of beers, engaged in an intense football debate. They were drawing up plays on napkins, that kind of thing. Suddenly, the door busted open and an assailant blew in with a shotgun and robbed the bartender clean.

Minutes later, the authorities arrived to file a police report. Asked his perspective on what happened, the bartender pointed at Saban and Stoops and said, "Don't ask those two a-holes. They've been so busy messing around on those napkins they didn't even know the robbery happened! Probably still don't!"

Saban cracked up retelling it. There you have it. The most applicable depiction of Saban's football focus, directly from the source.

That was it. Interview over.

Which was also when the conversation got interesting.

There were still ten or twelve minutes remaining on the commute, and after a brief silence Saban asked me where I grew up. I explained that I grew up twenty miles west of Blacksburg, Virginia, where Virginia Tech is located, in a little farm town called Pearisburg.

To my surprise, he was immediately intrigued.

Around this same time, news began to swirl throughout college football that legendary Hokies head football coach Frank Beamer would soon be relieved of his duties, or mutually agree to retire, or however you want to define that—so, soon, there would be new blood in Blacksburg.

Saban asked me how the Hokies' diehards were reacting. I explained that it was the natural, twofold response, that odd intersection where excitement meets nostalgia.

Coach Beamer built an empire. He took a proud football program, which in its history had largely underachieved, and ushered it toward being a national brand. Beamer Ball was a platform that a bunch of rural farm people could embrace and be proud of.

People from Carolina to California know where Blacksburg, Virginia, is. Frank Beamer is the overwhelming reason why.

But then there's the other side: It was time. Coach Beamer was getting older, and fair or not, folks had questioned for a couple of years if he was dedicated enough to extend himself to the utmost to ensure the program's competitiveness.

Saban nodded.

I kept talking.

In retrospect, I figure if we'd been anywhere else on earth other than Saban's car, I would probably have stopped the story right there. But we were driving. He didn't have anywhere else to go and I was on his time, so I explained to him why that intersection at which most VT fans found themselves did not apply to me.

To me, Frank Beamer was bigger than wins or losses or regional pride. For me, Frank Beamer was an extension of my father. Frank Beamer played an integral role in my relationship with my dad.

When I was young we weren't wealthy. We weren't poor, but we bought the 2-for-$2 ground round at the Food Lion every Saturday. My dad worked a lot. He wasn't around much in those days. So time with him was rare and fleeting. That made him mysterious, almost mythical, to my sister and me. But there were some rare Saturday mornings when he'd blow into my room, rustle me awake, and say, "Boy, get dressed. We goin' over the mountain."

That was code. That meant we were headed to Blacksburg to scalp a couple of five-dollar tickets, climb to the highest reaches of the west grandstands in Lane Stadium, and watch the Virginia Tech Hokies play football. It wasn't great football. Beamer hadn't built that empire yet. He was still laying bricks.

But none of that mattered to me. What mattered to me was spending time with Daddy, doing something he loved and seeing him from a unique perspective that erased some of the unknowns, while simultaneously adding to the mystique.

I rarely saw him loose and smiling. But when I was drinking a fountain Coke and eating a Reese's Cup, and he was yelling at the top of his lungs at the referee or the opponent, I swore I could touch the sky.

I had Daddy's attention. I felt his love and hoped he felt mine.

It was magical and important, and it forged an eternal bond yet to be broken.

Daddy died in 2008. I feel closer to him in Lane Stadium than I do anywhere else.

When I finished that testimony, Saban said nothing. A few moments later he hit me on the leg.

"I've lived it," he told me.

Saban was raised in Monongah, West Virginia. Marion County. The coal mines. Blue collars and dirty fingernails. Good people with good souls, good intentions, and proud last names. Food was on the table most nights. Not every.

In that area, hard work isn't appreciated. It's expected. It's just what you do.

Saban's old man, Nick Sr., owned a Gulf service station, just west of Monongah proper at Helens Run, where West Virginia Route 218 dead-ends at US 19. Nick Sr. used that gas station to fill tanks and hearts and bellies all over the region.

And he also used it, Coach Saban says now, to teach his son how to work hard and be kind when nobody was watching.

Years later, during one of the many championship media days at which Coach Saban was the star attraction, he described how his father used that town and those mines—and the principles they produced—to drive home a lasting lesson.

"Ms. Helminsky was my music teacher, and if it wasn't for her, I might not have been successful in life," Saban said during the 2018 National Championship media day in Atlanta, Georgia. He stifled a grin at the thought.

He continued: "Because she gave me a D in music when I wouldn't get up and sing, because I was shy. And my dad made me turn my basketball uniform in for getting a D. And he took me to the coal mines in West Virginia, and we went down 527 feet, and he said, 'This is where you're going to end up if you don't get an education.'

"So I made up my mind after that, that I'm going to do better in school."

That brought us back to the ride to work. He explained to me that once a year, his father would load the family in the station wagon and drive up State Route 19, which turned into Pennsylvania Avenue when they arrived in Fairmont, continuing on parallel with the Monongahela River until it became Main Street in Rivesville.

They would hook a left on First Street, which became Fairmont Road, and drive toward Westover before eventually arriving in

Morgantown. There, they watched the West Virginia University Mountaineers play football.

He then said the sentence that will forever define him for me, this coaching titan who has achieved historic dominance:

"I don't remember those football games…"

He paused, looking straight ahead out the windshield, tapping the steering wheel with his thumb.

"But I remember that time with my dad."

Nick Sr. died when Coach Saban was twenty-two years old. For his entire life, he wanted nothing more than to make his father proud.

The moment struck me, because I'd spent every day of my life trying to make my father proud. And it wasn't easy. He wasn't easily impressed.

So here I was, in this impossibly rare moment of fellowship with this mythical figure—about which I'm certain my father would demand every detail and be indescribably proud. And I'm certain he'd tell me so, too, because he would feel vicariously linked to Saban's greatness.

That would make him proud.

When I told Saban this, he nodded again. The air was quiet. It was a moment of vulnerability you'd expect from old friends, not a couple of guys who'd been acquaintances for twenty minutes.

It was bigger than either one of us and silently stripped any veneer from us both.

It was the power of a father's impact.

And for the lucky ones, like Saban and me, it is eternal and it is universal.

When we arrived at Saban's office, we exited the car and he scurried into Wednesday preparation for LSU.

And I wanted to call my dad.

Just one more time.

"Out Like That"

I'm not a songwriter by any stretch. Just wish I was. But it's not uncommon for me to jot down title ideas or lyrics. I do it all the time. "Out Like That" is from one of those moments where I was inspired to write by something I witnessed. I was on the couch watching the 2010 college football BCS National Championship game between Alabama and Texas. During the first drive of the game Texas's quarterback, Colt McCoy, was injured when Alabama defensive tackle Marcell Dareus hit him in the shoulder. His arm went numb and he was done. Boom. Over. McCoy had one of the best careers in college football history. He's a Longhorns legend. And there it went, out, just like that. I was corresponding with a songwriter friend of mine during that game, and I said, "Man, you ain't supposed to go out like that." He wrote back, "That's a song. Or at worst a good title. You write your side and I'll write mine, and we'll meet in the middle and see what happens." "Out Like That" is my side. Years later I drank a beer with McCoy at the Preakness Stakes and got to share this story with him. The shocked expression on his face was worth every minute of the wait.

Jesse James deserved to face that gun...
Number 3 deserved one more race won...
And those towers in New York...
Deserved to stand...
Cobain deserved one last show...
Lane Frost deserved one last go...
And I deserved one last day...
With my ol' man...

Chorus:

Some leave us way too early...
Leave in a flash...
Leave their mark on this world...
And then leave us way too fast...
They leave us wonderin' what mighta been...
Thinkin' damn was that a blast...
And why the hell did they have to go...
Out like that...

Dr. King deserved to live his dream...
Pawpaw deserved to reach Normandy...
Those kids at Sandy Hook...
Deserved to grow...
Lady Di deserved to see her hair turn gray...
For that matter so'd JFK...
And the *Challenger* deserved...
To come back home...

I deserve to see my children grow...
They deserve to see their dad grow old...
I deserve to walk my girls...
Down the aisle...

My wife deserves my everything...
My life deserves my every dream...
So I pray to my Lord...
I'll be around awhile...

Chorus:

Some leave us way too early...
Leave in a flash...
Leave their mark on this world...
And then leave us way too fast...
They leave us wonderin' what mighta been...
Thinkin' damn was that a blast...
And why the hell did they have to go...
Out like that...

Chapter Thirteen

Be Yourself

For Brandon Marshall, clarity was a plain white T-shirt and a yellow '71 Oldsmobile Cutlass 442. The car was flawless, with dual black rally stripes snaking the hood and a quartet of twelve-inch subwoofers thumping in the back glass. It provided the sensation of freedom, an open road, and a South Beach breeze ripping through the driver's-side window and across Marshall's chiseled face.

It was a moment of discovery, respite from a faceless captor, comfortable but not complacent.

This was a new Brandon. It took exhaustive effort to find him.

Marshall, then a wide receiver for the National Football League's Miami Dolphins, had recently completed a three-month outpatient treatment program at McLean Hospital in Belmont, Massachusetts, specifically tailored to teach coping mechanisms for impulsive reactions to adversity or frustration or depression.

Consciously, he was there to learn to control his emotions. Subconsciously, he was there to save his marriage and his career—and possibly even his life.

For the first five years of his NFL career, while playing for the Denver Broncos, Marshall's emotional outbursts defined him every bit as much as Pro Bowl production on the field did. And truth be told, to the average fan—and certainly to the casual fan—probably more. Negative headlines followed him.

Depression had him in its clutches. He didn't want to leave his house. When he did leave, he'd don a sweatshirt, drape the hood over his head, and pull the drawstring tight. He hid. He hid from friends, family, and teammates. He even hid from his wife. He didn't want to talk to anyone. He isolated himself, so desperately at times he would hole up in his home theater, turn off all the lights, and sit there in the dark, alone.

He was labeled a malcontent. He was labeled a troublemaker. He was a player with world-class talent and world-class output whose name always came with the "but…" In 2010 he was traded to Miami and handed the richest contract in league history at his position. Financial stability changed nothing about him emotionally.

Then in the summer of 2011, loved ones urged him to have a clinical evaluation, after which he was diagnosed with borderline personality disorder (BPD), which he describes simply as difficulty coping with and controlling emotions.

As he explained this to me, we were seated on wooden crates positioned at a chessboard in Brooklyn, New York, on the edge of the East River. It was a glorious late-August day in the summer of 2017; the iconic glass-encased Jane's Carousel merry-go-round lay before me, swirling laughter nestled on the pier between the Brooklyn and the Manhattan Bridges. It was 100 degrees. We were both wearing sweatpants.

Brandon tried to paint the borderline personality disorder picture for me using real-time context.

"You and I could be right here playing this chess game, and a guy could come up and flip over this chessboard," Marshall said. "We both get really pissed off, but it may take me longer to get back down to baseline—baseline being, let's move on.

"It may take you thirty minutes. It many only take you five minutes. Someone like me? If borderline personality disorder is in control—if I'm not in control of it—it may take me an hour. Maybe two hours. Maybe a whole damn week. The emotions we feel are valid. It's real. But the way we cope and manage doesn't come naturally to us."

For the professional athlete, impulsive behavior is both blessing and curse. Generally, the professional athlete, and certainly the football player, does not think. He reacts. But acceptable behavior between the lines can be considered barbaric and unacceptable outside the lines.

"The best players can't even describe that great play they made," he said. "It's like they black out. That Odell Beckham Jr. catch? The one-handed one we see every single day on the highlights? He can't tell you how he did that, or what was going on in his head. He can't!

"But in life, that doesn't work! You've got to slow things down. You've got to have critical thinking. And a lot of ballplayers, we don't have that."

That's why Marshall plays chess. It is a purpose-driven mental exercise in patience. It demands he consider the potential impact of every move and suppress his impulsive decisions. In his professional life, he is a modern-day gladiator, one of the planet's most macho individuals. They are taught to shun weakness, to suppress and mask pain. So the search for vulnerability can break them.

"It was the toughest thing I've ever done, to look at myself and say, 'Yeah, I am weak,'" Marshall said. "As football players, when we are hurt we say we're not hurt. So to finally come to terms and say, 'Hey, I am flawed, I am weak. I am hurt'—just to say that as a man is hard.

"A lot of times we get pissed off and display anger, and it's not that we're mad, it's that our feelings are hurt. Can you imagine saying, 'You know what, Eli Manning, you hurt my feelings.' The music would stop in the locker room! It's counterculture."

Marshall is a sweet man. He is a very smart man. I felt an instant connection with him, because I related to his plight. I, too, am impulsive. There have been countless times my switch was flipped and it could have cost me dearly. Trivial things like drunken bar disagreements or foul calls in rec-league basketball, all the way up the fallout scale toward critical moments in my professional life.

I balance that intensity with overwhelming empathy for others. I love people. I always have. With age and familial responsibility, I've learned to manage impulsivity very well. Ninety-eight percent of the time, I'm the easiest-going person. I'm quick to assist and champion others. I'm full of love and compassion and appreciation.

But even still, when I feel unjustly wronged, it takes conscious effort to quell the eye-for-an-eye revenge emotion. That other 2 percent bubbles up. It's just how I'm wired. It leads me to say things I don't mean sometimes. It leads me to react irrationally at times. I'm not proud of that. With age I've chilled way out. I am proud of that.

For as long as I can remember, when I make a mistake, the emotional reaction shifts instantly from heart-pounding anger to overwhelming remorse to the mission of righting the wrong. Within seconds, I jump through that range.

I'm admitting this because Brandon Marshall made me think about me, who I am and who I want to be. I'm not alone.

"I was the same guy before the diagnosis," he continued. "I deal with the same things. But I wasn't in control. I was out of control. The most powerful person is the present person—the person who controls what they can control. And I didn't. That's why my life was a living hell. When you don't know what you're dealing with, it's a moving target every day.

"I was always a woke person. I always looked myself in the mirror. I couldn't always control it all. But it was five years of hell. The first five years of my career was just one thing after another—over and over and over again. I knew I was a good person. But I always blamed it on the situation or the circumstances. I had to realize, the only thing we can control is what we can control."

McLean taught him control. For the first time in his life it wasn't someone else's fault. He was capable of admitting to himself his shortcomings and his failures. Before McLean, it was everybody but him—that coach, that player, that situation.

"The things we feel are valid," he said. "But the way we cope and deal with it is wrong. For me, it was always someone else's fault."

Then he said something I had never considered. Marshall grew up in Pittsburgh, Pennsylvania, in a community he says promoted impulsive behavior.

"I really feel like I was a product of my environment," he continued. "I feel like the etiology behind my disorder is environmental. You come to my neighborhood, you see a hundred kids like me, responding like me.

"Our grandparents respond the way I respond, or communicate the way I communicate, react the way I react. Aunts and uncles and moms and dads and teachers. You live in some volatile environments—very invalidating environments. I had to sit down and dig deep and really find out what life was about. And how it really works."

Marshall always knew he was a good man. After three months at McLean, he wanted to prove he was a changed man.

It was the fall of 2011, and Marshall was entering his second season with the Dolphins. While dressing at home before an early-season game, he was conflicted: What clothing ensemble would profess from the mountaintops the change within him? What outfit would define his evolution as a man? Everything about him had changed. How could he display it?

He tried on khaki shorts and button-down shirts. The mirror hated it. He tried a custom-tailored suit. It didn't feel authentic just then. Whatever Marshall sampled, nothing properly told his story. After an hour spent mulling over his attire, Marshall's wife, Michi, entered their room and found her husband in the closet. He asked her opinion.

"Just be yourself, baby."

Those words untied his binds, shielded the glare from his emotional windshield.

Just be yourself. It is fundamental. But like sports fundamentals, life's fundamentals require conviction and diligence and repetition to become muscle memory. If you pay them no mind and do not practice them, they can be your undoing.

It's easy to say, "Just be yourself," but very difficult to actually do it because most of us are tremendously insecure. Take something as frivolous as clothing, for example: How often do we dress for ourselves? Hardly ever. Unless we're in our own space at home, we dress for everyone else, to portray a certain image of what we want people to believe we are.

So when Michi told Brandon, "Just do you," it was liberating. This was the one person who mattered most in his life saying, "I love you no matter what, and I appreciate your determination to work tirelessly to find the man we both know you are and can be. Clothes? Who cares?"

Marshall placed a fitted baseball cap on his head and a white T-shirt on his back, kissed Michi, and jumped in the Cutlass. It was the perfect lesson: Let the world see change within your soul, through action and empathy and composure and security. All the stuff—clothes, cars, houses—is still just stuff.

"It was a defining moment in my life, in my marriage, in me," Marshall said. "I don't have to present myself like I'm this businessperson, this professional, when I'm not, just because I don't want people to look at me and say, 'That guy's crazy' or 'Something's wrong with him.' After I went to McLean Hospital, I was really struggling with my identity."

Uncovering vulnerability provided its own challenges for Brandon, namely on the football field.

"I've never been scared on a football field, ever in my life," he said. "But two months after I left McLean Hospital, I was on the field; I think we were in camp. I was just standing there, and a guy ran by me and I jumped. I was like, 'Oh my gosh, what was that?' It was a moment.

"I've never been fearful. I've always been courageous. And I found myself a different person on the field. I was a better man. But I was a different football player. I didn't have that thing that made me great, those emotions. I had the passion, but I didn't know how to control it. Because I knew that there was going to be four or five different cameras in my face, and any little bit of emotion I showed, everybody would be like, 'Oh yeah, that's borderline personality disorder.' And I didn't want that."

With time Marshall's purpose became unmistakable. Use football to change the world. Use football as a vehicle to change the narrative on mental health. Use the celebrity football gave him to become the face of that change.

"My purpose and my 'why' was because I loved football," he said. "The passion is still there. But it's second. I love the game at its purest form. This game saved my life. I was a kid from Pittsburgh, Pennsylvania; grew up in the neighborhood. If it wasn't for football, I wouldn't be where I'm at. So I love football and everything that comes with football—the life skills we learn along the way, the competition, the chase for greatness.

"But number one is the platform. I know football isn't my purpose anymore. I know the football field is a platform to be able to have a discussion with you and talk about my weaknesses and my vulnerabilities, because I know someone's always watching, and they're going to be freed because I'm showing them how vulnerable I am, and what I dealt with, and what I struggle with.

"And that person's going to seek help. There's been so many times where I've told this story and someone calls and says, 'Man, I planned on taking my life, but you gave me hope. And now I'm getting treatment.'"

Marshall wants to bridge the divide in the mental health community and erase the stigma that accompanies mental health–related diagnoses. Most individuals don't have access to the treatment that he believes saved his life. In three months at McLean Hospital, he spent more than $150,000.

"There's so many people out there hurting, but [who] don't have access to the coverage that I had. That needs to change," he said. "Hearing 'borderline personality disorder' was a relief. I was searching for a long time. It was hope.

"We like to say that you're not your diagnosis. That's not who you are. But to be able to be associated with something that can provide help and relief is one of the best feelings in the world. The three months after that was hell.

"It was hard work, with emotional days and days with tears shed. When you dive that deep into your flaws, so much is revealed. It was the most phenomenal experience I've ever had. I want to be sure others who need it, get it."

He credits Michi with ensuring his wellness. He says they were destined for each other. Michi is well studied in psychology. She is certified in behavioral forensics and behavioral profiling, and she holds a BA in psychology and a BS in criminal justice from the University of Central Florida.

She worked in the field before they were married and has her adult mental health first-aid certificate. She teaches youth mental health classes all over the world. Together, they founded Project 375, a nonprofit whose mission is to end mental illness.

"She was the fuel behind it all," Marshall said. "To this day she's the heartbeat of it all. She's a phenomenal woman. To go through so much—we've been through a lot—and to be a rock star in our community, and for our kids, she's phenomenal. It was hard, but if what we have now is the result of what we went through, I'd go through it all again.

"I think about that moment in the closet all the time, when she said, 'Baby, just be yourself.' I always thank her for that. It really helped me. I've been myself ever since."

We never got to finish that chess match. Someone came by and stopped it well before we were done. And neither one of us cared.

Bust

Ryan Leaf was a 1997 Heisman Trophy finalist, seated at the ceremony in New York City alongside Peyton Manning, Randy Moss, and the man who eventually won the award, Charles Woodson. By April 1998 Leaf was the number two overall pick in the NFL Draft, selected by the San Diego Chargers just behind Manning. Four troubled years later, he was out of the game altogether, viewed as a quitter and a malcontent, with the worst label possible: bust. Leaf later attempted suicide. He also went to prison. He had long masked his pain with substance abuse. What he did not know until much later, when he lost everything and sought help, was that depression was at the root of it all. On the Marty Smith's America podcast, Leaf detailed the moment he realized his career was over:

> I was at a place where I was just so sick and tired of being beat up, physically as well as figuratively, from the media and the critics clamoring in the background with the word *bust*. I also was depressed. I was clinically depressed. I hadn't addressed it. I had a really hard time staying in shape. I was embarrassed to show up to Seattle [training]

camp ten or fifteen pounds overweight, and get fired. That was a big mitigating factor for me, the embarrassment of that. There was a lot of depression there. There was a mental health issue, and at the time no one was really speaking out about mental health issues. What it said to people in the locker room was that I was weak and that I was lazy. And as I found out over time, depression can be so debilitating you cannot even get out of bed. You don't have the energy to go work out. I learned about this stuff after the fact. If I would have had the forward thinking to tell a team psychologist that I was struggling, maybe there was a path to a positive ending. But there was no outlet. I struggled with it. I thought I was weak. And my only answer to that was to quit—to quit something I wanted to do since I was four years old.

I've always had to look back on it and think, *Man, what a terrible mistake I made.* Especially with the stuff I know now, that there are treatments and assisted living–type things that could help me through that process. I just didn't even know they existed. I also didn't know what it was at the time. I just thought I was apathetic, and I was being told how bad I was and what a horrible person I was. And I tended to believe it. I still thought I had three pillars of success: money, power, and prestige, and that that would carry on regardless of whether I was playing. The prestige might be a little tarnished, but "former NFL quarterback" was good enough. Money was another drug. Before the substance abuse part of [my journey], money was the drug, and the power, and the fame of it all. The last thing I could do was show weakness to anybody. I couldn't go into a locker room and look my teammates and my brothers in the eye and say, "I'm hurting here, please help me!"

That was foreign. That wasn't seen. And we've seen a bunch of our brothers die over the past decade because of CTE [chronic traumatic encephalopathy] and mental health issues, because they were unwilling to ask for help. They thought their only way out was to take their own life. I was right there.

Chapter Fourteen

Workin' Hard to Get My Fill

A softball-sized lemon bundt cake rests before me on a plastic rainbow plate, white cream-cheese icing spilling from the top. Its shape resembles the head of a small jellyfish. It is my forty-second birthday.

I mention the cake-shape analogy to my then eight-year-old daughter, Mia, who is extremely perceptive and detail-oriented. She says it looks more like one of those mushrooms that perpetually try to foil Super Mario's sprint through his self-titled world. I don't disagree.

Stuffed atop the yellow spongy mound before me are two candles, side by side, both aflame. The one to the left is a yellow numeral 4, stippled with orange polka dots. To the right, a plum numeral 2, accented by violet polka dots. Damn, man. I am *forty-two*.

My children—Mia, her then twelve-year-old brother, Cambron, and her then five-year-old sister, Vivian—sit around the kitchen table, staring at their own mounds of confectionary bliss, served to them by Lainie, who is busy pouring milk and locating a grill lighter in the depths of the junk drawer beneath the phone. God bless her and all the moms. They make the world go 'round.

The kids are idling at that dicey moment where amped and exhausted intersect. It's an odd piece of real estate where the high meets the crash and the laughter steers abruptly toward whining before ultimately shifting into meltdown.

For this moment, we are happy. We have birthday cake and stories to share.

We just returned home from a successful visit to the Frye's Roller Rink, what certainly must be the last remaining roller-skating center in the universe. It is tucked away in the rural Charlotte outskirts town of Concord, known far and wide as foundational bricks in NASCAR's history, and appreciated by Gen-X Charlotteans because it is a time portal.

Stepping through the door at Frye's is like stepping into 1989.

The American roller rink is a dinosaur's habitat, still here and still glorious despite its inhabitants dying off in droves. Those that remain are the rarest of artifacts; ancient archaeological miracles speeding around in circles and dodging disaster on black and orange sleds, which upon removal overwhelm you with the fungal stench of a million sweaty feet. Their cargo parachute pants whip wildly as they glide, like wayward kites in a hurricane, offering a unique juxtaposition to their firmly tucked T-shirts, shoved so deeply within their pants you wonder how they breathe as they speed by, bobbing their heads and clapping their hands to whichever track from Journey's *Greatest Hits* screams from the low-slung speakers hanging from the end-zone ceiling.

Workin' hard to get my fill!

You can't help but be happy. Roller-skating is a unique brand of freedom in unbridled movement. Especially for kids. In this moment, my children are autonomous. Twelve, eight, and five, scooting solo around the glossy, hand-painted hardwood, Skid Row on blast, watching Mom and Dad grin like drunkards as we relive this last bastion of the eternal childhood rites of passage: the couples skate and the limbo and "Pour Some Sugar on Me" turned up to 11.

Follow me to freedom! Follow me to Frye's!

The sensation of untethered speed, dodging disaster, teetering on the precipice of a crash at any given moment, blinded by random flashes of disco light and bound by laughter, reminded me of how exciting it felt to be unleashed from my parents, dropped from a minivan full of rules and expectations directly into a world of my own opinions and decisions; sixth or seventh grade, when a childhood crush *actually let me hold her hand* for the first time.

Nothing feels like that. Ever again.

It transports you to the moment those songs hit you, to the concrete ledge of the riverbank, toes in the water and a towel over your head, sneaking nibbles of Chick-O-Sticks or Fun Dip as Kenny Loggins belts "Meet me halfway across the sky" on the boom box positioned in the window of the concession stand.

Forty-two. I'm not sure where the years went or why some of them are more memorable than others, why some are so vivid and some downright extinct like those dinosaurs, left to a story from a friend or a photograph in a box.

And as the candles burn and Lainie directs my children to begin singing "Happy Birthday," with all the wide-eyed wonder and innocence and limitless potential any parent could dream for, I can't help but consider the road to forty-two.

I've lived one hell of a blessed life. I have an amazing marriage and healthy children. I've seen Europe and Asia. I've stood on the Vatican steps and walked the Great Wall of China. I've met famous athletes and entertainers, attended fancy dinners, entered the White House. I still call my childhood friends. My friendships are many.

But as I sat there, staring through the candlelight at my sweet family singing to me, I was taken aback by the realization that few things feel quite the way true nostalgia feels, and how memories of our moments as children evoke unique emotions within us as adults.

Whether it's hearing a certain song from our youth, or happening upon a certain smell, or participating in a particular activity, we are instantly transported to real-time moments from bygone years. And we are intoxicated by the innocent emotions that accompanied those moments.

My hope is that my children will experience that sense of nostalgia someday, maybe at a wedding when they're on the dance floor and hear "Workin' hard to get my fill!" And maybe, as they dance and laugh, carefree, their minds will shift to a moment, twenty years prior, when they were speeding around Frye's Roller Rink with Mom and Dad.

And maybe the emotion they feel will be part joy and part sadness, but absolutely unique and special, like nothing else makes them feel.

Muriel Plays Piano

The stories and inspiration behind my favorite songs fascinate me. I search for those answers. I want to know who devised the concepts, who wrote which lines, what motivated those lines, and how those songs impacted or changed lives. One of those songs is "Walking in Memphis," written and performed by singer/songwriter Marc Cohn. That song is a hymn. Cohn detailed the inspiration for this timeless hit on the Marty & McGee program, a show I share on ESPN with my great friend and colleague Ryan McGee:

> "Walking in Memphis" is completely autobiographical. The highlights of the trip for me are also in the song. The bridge in the song says, "Reverend Green be glad to see you." Reverend Green is Al Green, the great soul singer. But I went and heard him preach at his own church, called the Full Gospel Tabernacle Church. Now, I'm a Jewish kid from Cleveland, but that experience was unparalleled in my life up to that point, musically and in every way. I was just crying in that church. And I got to meet Al Green

briefly, and years later I sang with him. So it was the beginning of a long journey that day.

The most remarkable part of the trip, though, was going to this place called the Hollywood, which I talk about at the end of the song. I mentioned Muriel. Muriel is a real person, a schoolteacher, sixty-five years old when I met her, and making some extra money at this little place where she sang gospel songs on Friday and Saturday nights, and she had a tip jar and made some extra dough. And I walked in there not knowing what to expect. But I immediately was drawn to this incredible woman, whose voice was like an angel singing these great gospel songs. And by the end of the night we were fast friends. And she invited me up to sing. And at the time I was searching for my songwriting voice. I wanted to be a writer in the worst way, but I only had a singing voice. I didn't have my own style of songwriting yet.

And Muriel and I started singing these gospel songs together, most of them I'd never even heard. She just fed the lyrics over my ear and I tried to catch up and sing with her. But at the end of the night we sang "Amazing Grace" together, and at the end she whispered in my ear, "Child, I think you can go home now, and write those songs you've been meaning to write." And that's exactly what happened. I came back to New York City, and all the sudden I had my voice. I wrote "Walking in Memphis" and "Silver Thunderbird" and "True Companion" and all these songs that, years later, I would get signed for to Atlantic Records. Muriel was the beginning of me finding my songwriting voice. That's another reason why I have no problem at all singing that song over and over. Because for me, way before

it was a hit, it defined for me my turning an enormous corner as an artist.

*One funny moment: After Cohn finished that remarkable story,
I bellowed that he should write it immediately. He laughed and
said, "Well, I kind of already did, didn't I?" Damn straight you did.*

Playing chess in Brooklyn with former NFL All-Pro wide receiver Brandon Marshall. This photo was taken the day I interviewed him extensively about his mental health battle with Borderline Personality Disorder. (August 22, 2017)

Nick Saban and Tim Tebow dig a fish hook out of my left shoulder on Saban's pontoon boat at Lake Burton, Georgia. An inauspicious start to a thought-provoking day with these two legends. (August 28, 2016)

The Smiths. From right: Leo, Joy, Stacy, and a thirteen-year-old kid with one of those $3 Barton's Barbershop flattop haircuts trying desperately to stifle the smile for which his mother begged and pleaded. (Circa 1990)

With my beautiful friend Olivia Quigley at the 2015 Special Olympics World Games in Los Angeles, moments after she won the 100M gold medal. She would win a pair of golds that summer, and inspire millions. (July 2015)

One of my first days covering college football. At Ohio State with Buckeye defensive legends, from left, Darron Lee, Raekwon McMillan, and Joshua Perry. In the days following this photo, these men would bring the national championship home to Columbus.

My beautiful family. I am so in love with them, and so proud of them. (December 2016)

Eric Church and me at that fishing tournament he wrote about in the foreword! We are kids, man.

Daddy was a titan. Hard as hell on me, demanding that I work for what I got. But unyieldingly supportive. I miss his guidance and zero-BS perspective. (Circa 1984)

With my high school football coach, Steve Ragsdale, and teammates Ray-pheal and Maurice Milton. We don't talk every day. But we are linked forever by the impenetrable brotherhood that is Friday Night Lights—and the lasting lessons learned between the lines. (September 2013)

Standing at the finish line of the 2014 Boston Marathon with my dear friend Brian Smigielski, Boston PD. What he did for me that day I'll never be able to repay. (April 21, 2014)

Ocean City, New Jersey, is a summer sanctuary for us. This photo is taken just off the boardwalk, where I was inspired to write "Beach Girl." Many of our sweetest memories live here and greet us upon arrival each beach season. (August 2018)

My grandparents' wedding photo, 1942. The Reverend James and Frankie Massey— Papa Jim and Mimi. A moment of joy before the horror he experienced during World War II.

Exhausted at the foot of the Grand Canyon with, from left, Marine Force Recon Platoon Commander Eric Kapitulik and Nebraska football coach Scott Frost. Worn out. And just getting started. (May 2018)

On the beach and across the board from Michael Vick in Hollywood, Florida, learning how deeply chess impacted Vick's life—and satiated his competitive drive while incarcerated at Leavenworth prison. (Summer 2016)

Moments after his final race, standing by his race car in Homestead, Florida, a celebratory Budweiser with my dear friend Dale Earnhardt Jr., live on *SportsCenter*. He—and Tiger Woods—loved it. (November 19, 2017)

The married couple mix tape. The simple letter Lainie left for me on my laptop that had a profound impact on me.

Chapter Fifteen

Chess Lessons

Mistakes. We make them. We're human and we're flawed. They can define us momentarily, and if dramatic enough can be life altering. Regardless of their magnitude, our mistakes will always be part of us. Like all experiences, they pinch at our artist's clay and reshape us into our current form.

Fortunately, we have grace. If we accept responsibility with genuine contrition and seek change, grace will buoy us—and in some cases even save us—and our mistakes do not have to define us forever.

I learned a lot about this from Michael Vick. Vick's mistakes are well documented. So is his penance. His story is a tale of poor decisions and their aftermath, of change and lessons learned and lives rehabilitated.

Vick is a phenomenon. Not *was*. *Is*. Before the fall, he was the most electric player in the National Football League, arguably ever. At quarterback, he was like an Independence Day fireworks show, brilliant and explosive and unpredictable. Every snap was a lit fuse on a Roman candle. Seconds between plays felt like minutes, hearts pounding in anticipation, building toward a limitless sky.

Set! Hut!

Boom! You stopped everything to witness the spectacle.

Vick was unstoppable in a league that habitually reduces the unstoppable to pedestrian. That's one reason it's so ironic that a stationary challenge—one that often penalizes speed and impulsivity—provides a microcosm of his life story.

Chess.

He beat himself. He went too fast and he lost it all.

"In life, you want to win," Vick said, thoughtfully choosing his words. It was spring 2016, and the former Pro Bowler sat across from me at a chessboard resting atop a bingo table on the Florida shoreline, in Hollywood. It was hot. Sweat crept down our brows and across our cheekbones as the sun wedged through the waving palm trees overhead, Vick's all-white Air Force 1 shoes half-buried in the sand beneath our feet. He was smart. He wore shorts and a T-shirt.

It was surreal sitting with him. I'd admired him for twenty years. I grew up in the shadow of Virginia Tech, a passionate Hokies fan. Michael Vick is the greatest Virginia Tech athlete ever. Somewhere deep in the closet, I still have a maroon jersey with a white 7 on it, bordered in orange.

He was happy to engage in a match and a chat, and he was antsy about the potential to earn one last season as an NFL quarterback. He'd spent 2015 with the Pittsburgh Steelers, won two of three starts and completed better than 60 percent of his passes. He felt he had proven his mettle as a quality backup, at minimum, and hoped to bring confidence and experience and the understanding of how to win to another NFL roster. Just one last ride.

He was thirty-five years old and had played football for most of those years.

"Football. It's been my ticket," he explained. "It's the reason I didn't end up full-fledged in the streets, or my life wasn't just thrown away. Every day I had something to dedicate myself to. That was the craft—getting better. It started out as a dream. There's not too many kids that can say they accomplish their dream in life."

Vick not only lived the dream. He lived a nightmare, too.

On the day we met, Vick knew his career was in its twilight. I mentioned that the sun might even be rising again. Because even though his shooting-star athleticism had begun to fade, his world was brighter. He smiled in acknowledgment—not acceptance, exactly—of that sentiment. Then he wrapped a left hand, once valued at $130 million, around the head of a pawn and moved it two spaces forward. Vick has a boyish smile. It is warm.

"When I started playing the game of chess, I always wanted to win," he continued. "It's important to make the correct moves in the game of chess. And it's important to make the correct moves in the game of life. Because one false move can be detrimental to your whole game."

Or to your whole life.

In December 2007, Vick was sentenced to twenty-three months in federal prison for his role in financing, facilitating, and participating in the underground but organized dogfighting operation Bad Newz Kennels in his hometown area of Surry County, Virginia. He served twenty-one months in the Leavenworth, Kansas, federal penitentiary.

Some folks will never forgive Vick for what he did to those dogs. They can choose not to accept his apology. But they cannot say he didn't try. They can question his judgment. They cannot question his desire to atone. When he filed for Chapter 11 bankruptcy—not Chapter 7, which would have enabled him to liquidate his assets and call it a day—in July 2008, he owed $17.6 million to his creditors.

He repaid $17.4 million.

Vick understands and acknowledges he was wrong. As he discusses it, there is regret in his eyes and shame in his posture. But he adamantly states that his life is a testament to the power of imprisonment.

He is rehabilitated. Today, he believes he is the best version of himself yet.

"The person I was before I went into Leavenworth didn't have a clue about what my life really meant to me," Vick said. "Now I'm passionate about gaining more trust in myself and my life as I move forward. I understand now that you can't take life for granted, which I did preincarceration. Now it's all being bottled up into one individual who has some direction."

Prison walls were the only barriers that could corral Vick, the only barriers capable of slowing his rocket-fueled trajectory long enough for him to consider the misguided life he was living.

"It's dangerous when you don't have any direction and you don't understand what's most important in your life, and how you don't think about the people that you affect when you don't make the right decisions," he said.

"Now I understand that. So it's always a pause. Postincarceration, man, I just came back a better individual from the time I stepped out. But I could feel myself making that transition while I was in Leavenworth, and that was part of my growth. They say prison is to rehabilitate, and I was one of the ones who got rehabilitated."

That's where chess comes in. Chess was a significant part of Vick's rehabilitation. Once inside, Vick didn't choose basketball to satiate his competitive drive. He didn't lift weights. He didn't run. He met an inmate named Dino, who ran the Leavenworth chess league with his friends. Vick watched, transfixed on the games, fascinated by the culture and the emotional attachment that accompany a one-on-one matchup.

Inmates sat for hours watching matches, learning moves, and considering strategy, sizing up the competition. Some chose against competing with others, Vick explained, for fear of being publicly embarrassed. Others were downright intimidating.

"They have all types of chess tournaments," he explained. "Guys take pride in being the best. Around eight, before count time, everybody's in the cafeteria, or in the chow hall, as we call it, playing with their partners. Everybody had a partner, somebody that they loved to play with or somebody who helped them hone their skills and make their game better. It was so intriguing."

He described the atmosphere as pin-drop quiet. Say nothing. Never give hints on a man's game. Some guys bickered. His greatest frustration on the board was once his greatest weapon on the gridiron— the unexpected move.

"I hated that part," he said. "I'm looking extra hard on the board to try to find something that maybe I don't see. But you get an audience, you tend to show off and you tend to move different. I wasn't high on that totem pole. There were some guys in there who were A1. Like, very good. Very smart. Very intelligent guys who could dismantle you on the chessboard."

He stopped his thought.

"I see you trying to steal!"

Vick caught me. I wanted his queen in my pocket early. It was an impulsive moment for me as a player. I would pay for it later.

I was thoroughly intrigued that Vick played chess. I love everything about the game. I learned to play in the fourth grade, when an older man in Pearisburg held after-school lessons at the Episcopal Church on Main Street, just down the block from the courthouse. I have no recollection of what prompted me to play.

The guy's name was Mr. Peters, and I distinctly remember his hands. His fingertips bent at the middle knuckle, toward his palm, almost in a constant grip, somewhat like forming the letter *E* in sign language. I presume he had arthritis, but I do not know that for certain. He would grasp the pieces not with his fingertips, but between his knuckles.

Mr. Peters was brilliant. All of my best friends in elementary school played, too, and we combined to make a decent school team. We would travel to tournaments all over the state. By high school, two of my friends, Jason Borillo and Mark Vinson—the latter of whom remains one of my best friends today, and who, incidentally, is now a Tampa Bay Rays athletic trainer—were top-five players in Virginia in our age-group. I was mediocre. I cared far more about Gary Payton than Garry Kasparov.

With age came greater clarity for me regarding the lessons chess teaches. Vick explained chess lessons well.

"First of all, if anybody explains the game of chess to you or teaches you how to play, it's got to be your elder," Vick said. "It has to be broken down and explained in a way where you can understand it and a way you can relate.

"These pieces are valuable. You have to learn to move them. And to me, every day is valuable. Time is valuable. Your thought process is valuable. I think kids have to learn that at an early age, learn to slow down. Don't move so fast.

"I mean, you get caught up in so many things that you wish you could take back or you wish you could do over again. But sometimes you don't get to do it over."

He looked at me and laughed.

"You don't get your queen back."

I knew what he was telling me. He was fortunate to get a do-over.

As Vick watched Dino and the boys compete in Leavenworth, there were so many pieces, which moved so many different ways to create a unique and different picture every time. Chess is a lot like life that way.

"I valued everything about it," Vick said. "And the patience that it taught me was the most valuable lesson. When you're incarcerated, patience is everything. You just want to go to the door and you want to break out. You want to run out. But you have to sit and take every step, every second, every minute, every hour, every day in stride.

"Surprisingly, playing chess made my time go by faster. Because my mind was sped up, even though the days weren't. So at the end of the day, when I looked up after fifteen games of chess, the day was over."

Chess demands great strategy and patience and foresight. As Vick improved as a player, he learned to better respect the opportunity and blessing his natural speed provided.

"Before I started playing chess, I'd never seen it that way," he said. "It just taught me to think before I act. Some things you do you just do it off impulse. You don't care about the reaction at the time, whether it's the reaction from the general public, reaction from family, reaction from friends, positive or negative. You just go for it.

"I just thought chess was an awesome way to compartmentalize everything that life, in general, entails. And it's serious. Very serious. That was the part that I really enjoyed about it."

He was accustomed to being the best athlete in every competitive arena he entered. This was different. He needed four full months of training and competition before he truly understood the countless intricacies of the game.

"That's the way life is, right?" Vick said. "It usually takes a while to get it."

Balance. Thoughtfulness. Consideration. Patience. Empathy. Appreciation. Stability. Respect. Perspective. Vick is learning.

"I wish I would have developed those traits earlier," he said. "It would have probably kept me distant, away from some of the things that I went through. But when I think back and I piece it all together, it all made me the man that I am today.

"I was blessed with the talent to captivate people. I'm so appreciative of everything. It's funny when I tell people this—I wouldn't change one thing about what I've been through. And I'm still growing as a person. That's the part about life that I appreciate—I'm still growing."

Michael Vick beat me on the chessboard that day. But I won, too.

He reminded me that loss can spawn victory, and failure can produce success. Despite personal disappointment in my failures, they contributed to the man I am. Which I believe is the most empathetic and appreciative version yet.

Chapter Sixteen

Hunter

Way up high in my closet, wedged in the space between the tallest shelf and the ceiling, well beyond reach from the floor and tucked away from sight, is a pair of golf shoes.

Those shoes are like dandelions in a bed of roses. They're not as elegant as their neighbors. But like a puffy white dandelion blossom, those golf shoes represent the promise of a wish.

The shoes are textured leather, white-and-brown saddle-style Nike spikes, size 11. The entire toe and the entire heel are white; the middle is brown with matching laces and precise white stitching around the perimeter. I recall wearing them just one time. On the 230-mile round-trip drive from Cornelius, North Carolina, to Darlington, South Carolina, to and from the funeral for the man who gave them to me—Jim Hunter.

Hunter is a NASCAR legend. In six decades in the sport, he held myriad positions, from track president to lead voice. With such intimate knowledge of so many spokes in the industry wheel, he was universally respected and adored in the garage, the media center, and the boardroom for his keen vision, quick wit, ceaseless kindness, and guidance.

He was like a character from a Faulkner book, Southern and sagacious and savvy and charming, a brilliant storyteller with an easy, disarming reaction to stressful moments. Dale Earnhardt's death in 2001 was NASCAR's darkest hour. The public relations staff was understandably overwhelmed and understaffed for a crisis of that magnitude.

Shortly after Earnhardt died, NASCAR appointed Hunter the chief spokesperson for the industry. He always knew what to say and how to say it, with an uncanny talent for speaking around difficult subjects. He knew NASCAR was on a global stage for unexpected and unfortunate reasons. The scrutiny was immense. He was never intimidated.

"We needed reinforcement," said Danielle Frye, a longtime friend, who in 2001 was the Winston Cup public relations director. When Hunter showed up in Daytona after Earnhardt's death, her staff numbered less than ten people.

"His impact was immediate," Frye continued. "The amount of knowledge he brought to our group was amazing. And the energy. From the time he entered his office in Building 5 in Daytona, he was nonstop. Maybe it was the cigarettes and Starbucks first thing in the morning. Maybe it was eating Carrabba's every other night. Or maybe it was his love, passion, and dedication to the sport that he adored. And believed in."

He immediately and methodically began redefining both the NASCAR and the driver PR groups. Before Hunter, the answer to questions from media was almost an involuntary "no." After Hunter, the answer was, at a minimum, "Let me check." That is a huge difference. It is the difference between feeling shunned and feeling heard. That grew a new trust between the media corps and the garage. Frye told me that watching him operate was "like getting a hands-on master's degree in public and media relations."

Hunter's wardrobe was 99 percent golf attire. Most days he

wore khaki pants, usually pleated; a white or pastel yellow, blue, or pink polo shirt underneath a black sweater vest with NASCAR's logo on the left breast; and golf shoes. He wore golf shoes everywhere, all the time. I mentioned it once. Three days later a box showed up at the house with a letter, including the signature "self-portrait" he included with every note—a swirly smiley face with a mustache.

"Wear these, BD! They'll help you write better, like me! Haha!"

"BD" was his nickname for me. I'll let y'all figure out what it stood for.

Before entering the NASCAR garage full-time, Hunter played football collegiately at the University of South Carolina and worked as a sportswriter at the *Atlanta Journal-Constitution*. He smoked like a chimney. He was a product of NASCAR's Winston Cup glory days, when cigarettes were as prevalent in the garage as motor oil. Back then, everybody smoked heaters. As a result, Hunter had an omnipresent Salem Light hanging off his lip or curled up in his left hand, waiting for fire. With his golf shoes and his sweater vest, he also wore a mustard-colored ball cap with "NASCAR 1948" stitched onto the front. That was his signature ensemble. His infectious laugh and easy self-confidence added to his aura.

Hunter's impact on me was incredible and indelible, personally and professionally. I am not alone. The only way I know to describe his impact is to analogize it to a sports coaching tree.

Great coaches produce what is known as a "coaching tree." The idea being that if the head coach is a tree's trunk, his assistants grow into his branches by progressing to head coaching positions themselves. They are offshoots of the head coach's philosophy and influence.

In NASCAR, Hunter produced more than a tree. He grew a forest. Generations of racers and reporters are indebted to him and carry his passion with them every day. That includes me.

My time with Hunter was special enough that I realized how special it was right there in the moment. He was one of those people whom everybody stopped to talk to, hoping to soak up his wisdom or hear a hilarious bygone tale about David Pearson or Junior Johnson. And here he stopped to embrace me. He used to say he saw a younger version of himself in me, someone who sought to build relationships with the athletes beyond the track. That was true. It is still true.

He often called me a throwback. To me that was the ultimate endorsement. It was his way of saying I was one of the boys, and that I could have hung with him and Pearson back in the '70s. He was a titan, a man of the people, a hell-raiser at heart. He used to print out articles I wrote that made him laugh or think or stew, mark them up in red ink, and mail them to my home—snail mail, with an envelope and a stamp—always including a handwritten note and that signature smiley face.

The most important thing Hunter did for me was believe. He believed in *me*. I was young when I entered the garage full-time. It was the height of alternative rock, and I bleached my hair and wore baggy pants. I was headstrong and thought I had it all figured out. I was running from something. Maybe my mom's death. I don't know. I had a different way of operating than most. I was immature and my writing was immature. But Hunter believed in the spirit of it. He saw my passion. I'm so grateful for that. If he hadn't, this book wouldn't exist. Because the stories within it would not exist.

I never aspired to be a television reporter. There are probably two reasons for that: (1) The written word was always my passion; and (2) I never considered TV plausible. Print journalism was my chosen major in college, and all I'd known professionally until a sunny spring day in 2006 when I received a cold call from an unknown number in the 860 area code. That call would typically have gone to voice mail. I don't often answer calls from unknown telephone numbers.

I'm not certain why, whether it was boredom or Jesus, but this time I answered.

"Hey, Marty, this is Jack Obringer, from ESPN."

That moment is very clear in my memory. Time stopped. I was driving home from Costco, north on Interstate 77 in my black Chevrolet Silverado. A vanilla sheet cake—white icing with baby-blue trim—sat on the bench seat behind me. My vocal five-month-old son, Cambron, faced backward in an infant carrier, lying right beside the cake. The music was up and the windows were down. That's what I did when my kids were upset in the truck: I cranked some country music to reduce the anxiety. Theirs and mine.

It was a pretty morning. One of those spring days that act as a corrective lens, injecting vividness and clarity into the blur of winter. I rolled the windows up and asked for whatever was just stated to please be restated.

"Hi, Marty, this is Jack Obringer with ESPN. I'm a coordinating producer and wanted to chat with you off the record about a potential position here."

Somehow my mouth formulated and responded a composed "Yes sir," while my mind hollered a bewildered, *What the hell? Hell yeah you can!*

I wouldn't have been more shocked if Jack had told me I won the lottery. In a way, he did. His call was every bit a winning ticket.

Jack, who would become one of my most trusted mentors at ESPN and remains so to this very day, explained that in 2007 the network would reenter the NASCAR broadcast space, having purchased the rights to televise the second half of the Cup Series season and the entire thirty-five-week Nationwide Series season, through the conclusion of the 2014 campaign.

He explained that I might be a candidate for a NASCAR

"Insider" position, which, basically, was a working title for a well-connected reporter who knew the inner workings of the garage and could break news stories or confirm reports from competitors. That was an ESPN trend for a while—take print writers, inherit their contact and source bases, and mold them into TV newsbreakers. It was quite a transition. They let us learn on the fly.

Sitting on your couch watching Tom Rinaldi spit out flawless forty-five-second live reports from Augusta or Athens, informative and detailed, looks simple. Trust me, it is not. When you're standing in front of that camera, aware that the entire country is watching, and the red light turns on, and your eyes widen and your heart rate increases, and your field producer—standing right beside the lens—points at you, and a show producer you can hear but cannot see hollers, "*Go!*" in your ear, and talks to you while you're talking to America? There is nothing simple about that. Folks like Tom just make it look easy.

It takes time and repetition to find confidence and relaxation in that moment, and to learn the verbiage and the cadence required to succinctly but dynamically share information. For me it was a comedy of errors at first.

Example: At the Daytona 500 in 2007, there was a huge news story. NASCAR had cited driver Michael Waltrip for using an illegal substance in his engine. This was also Waltrip's first race as a team owner, as well as Toyota's first foray into the Cup Series. Huge story. We went live immediately.

Jack cued the microphone during one of my reports on the matter, with the instruction to finish my thought and then toss it over to another reporter, Angelique Chengelis. "Toss it" is TV-speak for finding a nice transition to set up the next reporter for his or her commentary. Typically, it goes something like this: "Now, for NASCAR's response to this situation, here's so-and-so."

My mind simultaneously worked to formulate accurate words

regarding this important news story, while also working to determine an eloquent toss. It was not eloquent. I simply repeated Jack's instructions verbatim, on national television: "Okay, now I'm going to toss it over to Angelique for her report." We still laugh about that.

Before I left NASCAR.com for ESPN, I wrote mostly features and debate. Not much breaking news. I had dabbled in TV, providing sporadic studio analysis and reporting. In 2005, Speed Channel got a wild hair and produced a ten-week program called *Backseat Drivers*, during which I debated pressing NASCAR topics with my friend Shannon Spake (who is now a big star at the FOX Network). I hope I never see that footage. We were both young and driven. But when it came to making television, we were as green as St. Patrick's Day.

Surely, Jack had called the wrong person. I actually told him he had the wrong guy.

I have a colleague named Marty Snider, a talented and versatile NBC broadcaster who covers everything from the Olympics to the NBA to NASCAR, and for whom I am sometimes mistaken. Marty and I laugh with each other often about how many people call him "Smith" and me "Snider." Therefore, I figured that *had* to be the redheaded "Marty" Jack was aiming for. I told Jack I had Snider's number and could supply it if he wished.

He laughed out loud and ensured me he'd called the right guy. I would later learn why: The most influential endorsements came from ESPN's in-house NASCAR reporter, Mike Massaro, and Jim Hunter. Those men changed my life.

I was very comfortable as a writer. It was fun and I was good at it. But ESPN doesn't call every day. So despite legitimate concern about leaving my comfort zone, I accepted the job the moment it was officially offered to me.

I would rather crash and burn and fail *knowing* I'm not capable, than wonder years later if I should've tried.

When I was a young reporter in my early to midtwenties, clueless and wild as a mountain lion, Hunter grabbed me up under his wing. This was the early 2000s. His tutelage included life lessons disguised as professional guidance. Things like negotiating garage politics and relationship-building. He had made a career of both, and he took time to show me how.

He would walk into racetrack media rooms all over the country, sidle up beside me, and ask me to go take a walk. We'd stroll through the Cup Series garage, wave at every passerby—because he knew them all—and make our way to the NASCAR transporter, an 18-wheeler that was outfitted to serve as the sport's garage command center. They called it "the Hauler."

Inside the Hauler there were cabinets running the entire length of the trailer, top and bottom, which held two-way radios used to communicate during competition, computers that tracked car data, and paperwork. There was a refrigerator, and a countertop placed between the top and bottom rows of cabinets. I probably stole a thousand Little Debbie Oatmeal Creme Pies and FireBall jawbreakers from that display.

When I first started in NASCAR, the summer of 1999, one of my jobs was to set up a garage camera that I bolted to the top of that trailer, on the right-rear corner. It was stationary and provided a view into the garage area for the NASCAR.com user. It was revolutionary technology at the time. To get it running, I arrived at the track on Thursday afternoon, entered the trailer, and climbed up a ladder and through a hole barely wider than I was, wedging myself into a tight space between the floor and the ceiling to connect a modem, a phone line, and coaxial cables. It was very important to my bosses, and therefore gave me tremendous anxiety. I was embarrassed to ask for help. I thought I was bothering people. What it ultimately did was ingratiate me to the sport's crew of officials. I had to keep the same schedule they kept, which was before the garage opened until after it closed. They respected that, and it forged friendships that still exist today.

Anyway, Hunter and I would walk past the snack station and the fridge to the trailer's lounge up front and sit awhile, and he would explain some of the sport's pressing issues to me from his—read: NASCAR's—point of view. The insight from those conversations had a distinct way of shaping the thoughts I wrote on those topics. Sitting in that lounge—which had black leather couches, wall-to-wall mirrors, a wall-mounted television, and a countertop with laptop computers tracking practice times for the drivers—also meant I was positioned among other NASCAR executives or drivers in private settings, where important matters were discussed and hilarious stories were shared. Those did not make their way into print.

Hunter trusted me and everyone else trusted him. As a result, I attended a sort of stock car college, held in that lounge or in back rooms at racetracks or behind closed doors in motor homes parked at the racetrack. These moments were as much about social and personal growth as they were about racing. He gave me that.

My sweetest memories with Hunter were the evenings when it was just him and me in the bronze motor home he lived in at the track. Or just us and his best friend, Herbert Ames. Herbert was a larger-than-life character, like Hunter, a proud South Carolinian, rotund and always talking, and most of the time talking trash. (He would love that those words are in this book!) Those two were straight from *Grumpier Old Men* central casting. They fought and bickered and belittled each other constantly, and the laughs that ensued were a beautiful song. They were inseparable—Hunter calculated; Herbert unbridled.

We'd sit inside Hunter's bus, and I'd drink some cheap beers bummed from campers outside, and he'd light one Salem off the next and tell me stories about the old days. Again, Hunter was a product of the bygone NASCAR era when R.J. Reynolds Tobacco Company out of Winston Salem, North Carolina, breathed life into a choked-down sport, stamping its iconic red, white, and gold Winston branding on the walls and souls of every racetrack and race driver from Florida to California.

The NASCAR Winston Cup Series. God that sounds beautiful. I can still hear the great NASCAR broadcaster Bob Jenkins say it in my mind, along with the location and the sponsor of that day's race. It was the only time we got to see the sport: the actual race. There was no internet or social media.

Welcome to *ESPN SpeedWorld*! Today, live from North Wilkesboro Speedway in North Carolina, the Brushy Mountains looking on, for today's Tyson Holly Farms 400...I'm Bob Jenkins alongside Ned Jarrett and Benny Parsons, and we'll have all the action for you today.

It was music. As Sunday mornings ticked toward noon, my dad and I leaned hard on the edge of the pew at Pearisburg Baptist Church, waiting anxiously for the preacher to say the final amen. We'd hop up, high-five the pastor on the way out the door to the truck, fire it up, and rush home to catch the green flag and kickoff. Mom and Stacy would catch up later.

We had a tube TV in an entertainment hutch my grandfather built, cherrywood, atop which sat one of those beige boxes shaped like a loaf of bread, that used a slide-rule channel guide, 1 to 36, every third number in script and the others denoted by black dots. Daddy would turn to me and say, "Boy, turn it to Channel 7."

Like most kids back then, I was a human remote control. I hated it. I thought, *Why don't you get up off your ass and change it to Channel 7?* But I didn't dare say a word. I got up and changed it to Channel 7.

In my mind, little nowhere towns called Martinsville and Wilkesboro and Darlington and Rockingham were the grandest locations, arenas hosting steel-horse gladiators named Earnhardt and Allison and Elliott and Rudd. Back then NASCAR hadn't yet undergone the explosion into the mainstream it would later experience.

This was the '80s, before Earnhardt and Jeff Gordon became the oil and water that mixed to fuel a phenomenon and lift the sport from the backwoods into the American consciousness. Earnhardt's black number 3 and Gordon's rainbow-painted number 24 were diametrically opposed in the minds of their loyal and passionate fan bases, creating an explosive rivalry from which they got very rich, and made everyone else very rich in the process.

The boys weren't as wealthy then, though. And when grown men with rough edges are fighting—often literally—to keep lights burning and bellies full, they'll push to the physical and emotional extreme to succeed. That's what built NASCAR, that raw emotion, which carried a hint of desperation when it raced through the television sets and into our living rooms.

In some cases it was hatred and the willingness to do whatever it took to win. It wasn't about friendship or sportsmanship. It was about paychecks. And there was a primal appeal to that. It was raw and authentic. Dirty faces and grimy hands. The fearlessness to drive hell-bent into Turn 1 with no guarantee you'd make it out the other side.

That era fascinates me. I wish I'd seen it in person. There are lifers still in the sport today, whom I greatly admire, genuine and kind and eager to share stories about the glory days. One of those folks is Hank Jones, Earnhardt's merchandise man back in the '90s, when the merchandise industry became an untapped oasis, a boon, a printing press for money, as T-shirts and ball caps and bumper stickers and bottle openers and every other damn thing you could possibly imagine flew off the shelves.

Hank looks like a Bocephus song. Black shirt, black hat, black Wranglers, black shades. He lived it and lived to tell about it. And as the sport has evolved away from its roots, he desperately wants to tell about it.

The NASCAR garage can be difficult as hell to navigate. Entrance points aren't readily accessible. But once you're in, you tend to stay in. I remember distinctly how intimidating it felt when I first began working in the garage. Everyone seemed to know everyone else, and I knew no one else. There seemed no possible way to ever know all or any of these people, on all of these race teams, which are really minifamilies in a 200-mile-per-hour traveling circus, all hugging one another and saying hello and flipping the bird and breaking bread. It was sensory overload. And it was impossible to rationalize.

Hunter helped me. He knew every angle of the sport: the governing body, the race teams, the drivers, the fans, the racetracks, the sponsors, and the media. He's the only person I've known who had everyone's perspective at all times and was actually sympathetic to those perspectives. I hung on every word he shared in that motor home or at the dinner table about guys like his buddy Pearson or his close friend Bill France Jr., the namesake heir to NASCAR founder Big Bill France's throne, who took his father's vision and led the sport to explosive growth and popularity.

We'd sit in that bus and Hunter would tell me about fried chicken and Budweiser parties with Junior Johnson at Darlington Raceway. I'd share stories about the Saturday morning shower line in the Talladega infield, standing beside a guy with Earnhardt's signature number 3 tattooed on his butt, who waited for the perfect tranquil moment to holler "EARNHARDT!" at the top of his lungs through a gasping laugh that reverberated off the cinderblock walls. Or I would sparingly detail what I remembered about racing Jimmie Johnson on mobile barstools after ten or twelve beers, and tumbling down in his front yard toward Lake Norman. Johnson wore a skateboard helmet. I wore a football helmet. I do remember that. Hunter found that visual hysterical.

He'd sometimes laugh so hard at my exploits that the Salem smoke shot out his nostrils like a stick of dynamite had exploded in his nose. All those belly laughs left a beigy nicotine stain on his white mustache, right under his nose. I loved that stain. It was a part of Hunter's character and reminded me of my daddy. Dad had a similar stain on his white, Wilford Brimley–style mustache.

I think in many ways Hunter reminded me a lot of my dad.

If you ask most any driver who raced from 1960 to 2010, Hunter likely played a role in his or her career, some more pivotal than others, of course. Intense competitors like Kevin Harvick, Kyle Busch, and Tony Stewart owe Hunter greatly for their extended success—which will most certainly land them all in the Hall of Fame someday.

Harvick, who is always direct in analysis, explained Hunter's impact this way: "If it wasn't for Jim Hunter, I probably wouldn't be in NASCAR today. I was in so much trouble [as a young driver], nobody wanted to deal with me, and Jim was the common ground that helped me reestablish relationships within NASCAR. Jim didn't always agree with me, but he always listened. He had his own unique way of explaining what I needed to do, yet letting me remain true to myself."

In October 2001, at the Talladega Superspeedway, NASCAR mandated that all drivers must wear one of two approved head and neck restraints, to prevent the head from snapping forward in an accident. This was one of the many aftereffects of Earnhardt's death. Nearly every driver had already implemented this tactic well before the mandate. Stewart, meanwhile, had not.

Hunter adored Stewart. The throwback effect. He appreciated that Smoke—Stewart's nickname in the garage—spoke his mind and did things his way, outside opinion be damned. Stewart was decidedly old-school. If he thought one of my questions was stupid, he told me it was stupid. He does not pander. Ever. He reminds a lot of people of Earnhardt.

Hunter and Stewart talked often. He was a voice of reason for Smoke when NASCAR's decisions were confusing. They debated often. One of those debates centered on those head and neck restraints. Stewart ultimately chose to assimilate. His chats with Hunter were at least one reason why. That demonstrates the respect Hunter carried.

When relationships grew contentious between competitors or, more regularly, between the governing body and the media, Hunter was the mediator and the peacekeeper. Especially in those weeks and months after Earnhardt died.

"Even before February 2001, we knew we needed that perfect voice, and we didn't have the voice we needed," former NASCAR president Mike Helton told me. "That's when we pulled Hunter back into the fold. He could talk to the industry—and listen to the industry—and bring that information back to us, and be a voice of reason from our side.

"Because everybody wanted to know how something like [Earnhardt's death] could happen. We didn't have all the answers. We knew we had to give answers, but in the meantime we had to manage all the crucial relationships. He was *the guy* capable of doing that."

From that time until Hunter got sick with cancer, Helton leaned on Hunter in difficult moments.

"Every time I had a tough relationship with a driver, owner, or crewmember, because of rules or regulations or personality conflicts, I called Hunter." Helton laughed as he continued, "I'd be the bad guy, then call Hunter to go smooth it out as the good cop, so that person didn't hate everybody in NASCAR. He was so great at that."

I once made Hunter laugh so hard he nearly swallowed his Salem. The way his lip curled around his cigarette when he laughed was beautiful. Most times he would laugh and never touch the heater. It would just bounce up and down on his lip like a teeter-totter. It was magic. This time he almost inhaled it. And it was lit.

I was recalling to him my introduction to his best friend, former NASCAR chairman Bill France Jr.

It was May 1999, and I'd just been hired by NASCAR to work for the league internet site, called NASCAR Online. I attended races, interviewed drivers, arranged those damn phone line connections to produce live practice timing and scoring charts on the website, and set up the camera on top of the Hauler. I was twenty-three years old.

Prior to joining the company, I had to attend an orientation of sorts at the NASCAR headquarters in Daytona Beach. When I arrived I was terribly nervous. I checked in at the front desk and paced while waiting to be summoned. I walked into the lobby bathroom. I'd never seen a john like this, all brass and marble. I stood at the urinal, awestruck, using the bathroom.

The door opened. Bill France Jr. walked in.

I was conflicted. *Do I say hello? Chat him up?* What's protocol when you don't know someone, but you've been a lifelong admirer of that person, and you're both holding your privates in your hand? I decided to go for it.

"Mr. France, I can't tell you how much it means to me that you'd believe in me. I've been a fan my whole life, and it's an honor beyond description to represent your company. Thank you for this amazing opportunity. I won't let you down."

Mr. France did not look up. I expected he was preparing an impassioned response of welcome and wisdom. He began to speak. I expected to be inspired.

"Who the hell are you?"

Hunter loved that story. He would ask me to tell it and retell it in all types of company, from the most distinguished guests to the simplest. Every time I told it, he laughed so damn hard he bounced. I miss that laugh. And I miss his perspective.

As I reflected on his influence, I wondered what he saw in me. I asked Jack Obringer, another of my mentors, the ESPN executive who made that initial phone call way back in '06.

"Hunter was one of the first NASCAR people I got to know," Jack said. "NASCAR had given me a couple of candidates, but none of those suggestions panned out. Hunter tells me he's high on this kid who writes for the NASCAR website. Good writer, hungry, has good relationships with the drivers—and more than a heaping spoonful of personality. And then when I met you, I remember you had some natural fear of the unknown—you had done precious little TV. But I would suggest I was really drawn to your personality, and that you were simply comfortable in your own skin."

That's a trait Hunter had, too. He died in 2010 after a yearlong battle with cancer. He was seventy-one.

"He created so much humor for all of us, because he was so good at laughing at himself," Helton said. "That endeared him to a lot of people in your generation, who leaned on him for advice and guidance. That was a great resource."

One of my greatest.

"Old"

Teens just want to fit in. Social acceptance drives the narrative of adolescence. Our friends shape our interests. We speak like our friends and dress like our friends in search of gaining more friends or, more importantly, preventing the ones we have from mocking us. And that, inevitably, results in some unfortunate decisions in the ways of slang-speak and fashion, decisions on which we look back and wonder what we were thinking. And memes constantly appear on the internet to remind us just how unfortunate those choices truly were. For me it was tight-rolled, acid-washed jeans and a minimullet. Or attending prom in University of Michigan basketball shorts. That actually happened. I was a big Fab Five fan. In the early '90s, that group of Wolverine freshmen captivated the entire nation—even farm boys in Nowhere, Virginia. There was a sports apparel mailer magazine called Eastbay that sold baggy college basketball shorts. Authentic. I saved up some hay money and bought a yellow Michigan pair with the block navy M. The waist size was 44. I was a 28. Maybe a 28. And I wore them to prom with some black-and-white Nike Veer cross-trainer sneakers, the signature *shoe of NFL Hall of Fame defensive end Bruce Smith at the time. Somehow—and I have no idea how—my parents did not ridicule me or try to change my mind. They just laughed. (I always heard a rumor that in the aftermath of that debacle, the Giles County school board created a rule to outlaw shorts at prom.) Many (most?) teen fashion decisions bewilder parents. But if they're harmless and not terribly revealing, we tend to shrug them off as part of the exploration process of who we are in that moment and who we want to become. I was reminded of that when Cambron received a North Carolina Tar Heels hat, camo with a Carolina blue interlocking N-C, which I wore in a pinch and, out of habit, folded the bill to shape it away from its cardboard-stiff origin. Cambron was not thrilled. "Dad. I don't bend my hats. I like the flat bill." Instantly, I realized I'd become my dad.*

Old

It's not cool to bend your hat...
These days the kids all wear 'em flat...
When I was fifteen it wasn't like that...

Their hair swoops low across their face...
My old man would scream disgrace...
But I'd beg him to differ...
That's not the case...

Kids are young and want to be bold...
Stand up tall against all they're told...
We were all that way once...
Breaking the mold...
And then we got old...

Chapter Seventeen

Be a Light

The mattress, once white, was dingy now; soiled gray and stippled with faint brown dots that blended like freckles. It was suspended vertically in the center of a garage, hammered at its fringes into the ceiling and the floor by nails and staples and straps and pins, and whatever else might fortify it from the onslaught.

The garage door behind it was equally blemished, its aluminum face dented with pockmarks from the constant abuse. The ceiling above was destroyed.

The mattress was a fortress and a fantasy. It was both vehicle and avenue, entrance and barrier. The beatings it withstood inside offered its abusers refuge from what lurked outside.

It was the Road Hole at St. Andrews and the island green at Sawgrass. It was 18 at Pebble Beach, imaginary waves from the Pacific crashing into a seawall by the fairway. For hours each day, two young boys hit ball upon retread ball into the cushioning and let their imaginations take them away from the chaos to exotic lands all over the world.

It was number 16 at Augusta National in 2005, and the boy

played the part of his hero, Tiger Woods, fist pump and all. Chip. Roll. Stop. Swoosh. Drop. Bedlam.

In the quest to follow Woods onto the PGA Tour and into superstardom and a better life, the mattress would provide Tony Finau a different kind of Amen Corner.

"Oh, man, yeah, it was Amen Corner a lot of days," Finau said of the mattress. "It was every hole at Augusta; the hard draw on 13, hitting the tee shot on 11, roping one down there.

"It's quite funny. I'm known for my [driving] length. And in that garage, we'd always have a driving contest. It's all about the sound. I'd smash one and say, 'That flew 320!' And my brother would get up there, hit it, and yell, 'I flew that 350!'

"We never knew who hit it farther. But I do know this: When we got out of that garage and away from that mattress, the ball flew forever when we hit it. So we definitely did something right."

Finau told me this on an unseasonably warm Georgia morning in March 2018, three weeks shy of his first career start in the Masters Tournament at Augusta National Golf Club. When Finau entered the room, dressed in all black, long and lanky, a golfer in a basketball player's body with a thousand-watt smile and the easy posture of a contented man with a specific if not unfulfilled purpose, I had no idea he would so deeply impact my life.

Learning Finau's purpose would speak directly to my own, in a way I'd long hoped something could. I'll explain how and why in a moment. But before you can understand how well he articulated my truth, you must first understand the journey that led to his purpose.

As we chatted, Finau's anticipation of the Masters was palpable, wrought with appreciation and balanced by the acknowledgment that a relentless work ethic and chance meetings cut his unorthodox path.

"I came through a very small window to get here," Finau said.

"Looking back now I can see that window was closing on me. I got on tour when I was twenty-five. The standards these days, that's late. A lot of these guys are winning at twenty, twenty-one years old. Stars are born by twenty-five. So my window was closing."

He shunned an opportunity to play collegiately at Brigham Young University, lured by money toward the professional ranks. And at age seventeen he bet on himself—he turned pro the day he graduated from high school. For six years he played anywhere at any time, on all manner of minitours across the United States. In 2009 he nearly won the made-for-TV Golf Channel competition called *The Big Break*. It paid $100,000 to the winner. He finished second.

Meanwhile, during that same six-year grind, he married and had a son. As if the chase isn't stressful enough.

Anxiety was high and the bank balance low. It nearly broke him. But Finau refused to let doubt thwart his faith. During low moments emotionally he leaned heavily on a deep Mormon faith, and he often considered how far he'd come from that soiled mattress in that frigid garage.

"I knew I belonged on the PGA Tour—I'd seen enough of my game to have no doubt," he said. "And I'd worked so hard for it; hours and hours in that garage. We go back to our childhood apartment, and the golf-ball dents are still all over the garage door, all in the roof. We left our mark on that place. It's incredible, actually."

Finau's story is nothing short of incredible. He grew up in the Rose Park projects of Salt Lake City, Utah, the third of Kelepi and Ravena Finau's seven children. He described an environment where drugs, gangs, and violence were everywhere around him. That concerned his parents. Kelepi, Tony added, feared the streets would beckon his young sons, Tony and Gipper, to the crime and deviant behavior that had stripped the promise of many of their peers. So he sought unique ways to distract them.

Many boys in Rose Park turned to sports—basketball and football mostly—for recreation and an emotional outlet, and for status and for some hope of a way out. That included family: Finau's cousins, Haloti Ngata and Sione Pouha, would both make it to the National Football League. Another distant cousin, Stanley Havili, went to the University of Southern California on a full scholarship. And yet another cousin, Jabari Parker out of Chicago, would star at Duke and become the second overall pick in the 2014 NBA Draft. Tony, too, could have chosen basketball. He received scholarship offers from multiple universities.

But if pro ball was ultimately the goal, the numbers on the field and the court weren't in Tony's favor. The fields and courts throughout Salt Lake were constantly buzzing with participation, hundreds of kids, just as they were in countless other cities and towns across the country. So Kelepi, a baggage handler at the Salt Lake Airport earning a $35,000 annual salary, formulated a plan that was foreign both to Rose Park and to his own beloved Polynesian culture: He would mold his sons into golfers.

"I don't know how he did it," Tony said. "No idea. The man is a visionary, a genius."

Mad scientist, maybe. The PGA Tour had no Polynesian players at the time. Kelepi did not personally play the game—couldn't afford to—and hadn't the slightest idea how to get started. But Tiger, a black man with Asian heritage, was dominating the Tour and challenging the establishment with unprecedented ferocity. With that came hope and inspiration and determination for millions of impressionable youth, including Tony and Gipper Finau. Kelepi saw their wonderment. He would find a way.

Admittedly clueless but undaunted, Kelepi went to the library and borrowed a reference book called *Golf My Way*, written by legendary golfer Jack Nicklaus. It provided a textbook and a road map for his sons. He then went to a thrift store and bought Tony and Gipper each three secondhand golf clubs at seventy-five cents per club, took them home, chopped them down, and rebuilt them to junior size. He piled the boys in the car and drove them past the fields and the courts and the gangs and the guns—to the golf course.

"My dad put me in the situation—with the understanding of the situation—that team sports are the attractive sports when you're a kid," Tony continued. "Because when I was a kid golf wasn't that cool.

"But Dad said, 'Look, let's grind our teeth in this game and see where it takes us. We have absolutely no idea what we're getting ourselves into, but let's just grind and see. No matter what, it's better than the streets.' And he was right. And I'm so glad I listened to him."

Kelepi visited the local municipal golf course and quickly realized how expensive the game was to play. But he also learned that the practice green was free. The boys could chip and putt all day long, expense-free.

And that's what they did. They chipped. With three sawed-off clubs and a bucket of haggard second- and third-hand golf balls, scraped from the woods and bummed from neighbors, from the school bell through the dinner bell, they hit "millions of chips," Tony said. It benefited them greatly. It demanded that their golf swings become an exercise in sound, not feel.

That same philosophy applied to the driver. And the mattress.

"Coming from Utah, we could only play six months out of the year—maybe seven if we were lucky," Tony said. "My dad is an incredible athlete, and he knew if we were going to excel at anything, we had to play all year round.

"So in the wintertime he set up a mattress inside the garage and attached it to the ceiling. I hit on one side. My brother hit on the other side. So we could hit simultaneously into the mattress.

We would hit off of a really thin piece of carpet, and underneath the carpet was cement. That's how we trained in the wintertime.

"My dad knew if I was going to compete against kids in California, kids in Texas and Florida who have the weather, I was going to have to sharpen my skills year-round. So for those four or five months every year, we hit into the mattress. We learned how to strike a golf ball inside that garage. We didn't have the funds to have a professional coach, didn't have funds to fly to California and play and practice. So we had to figure out a way.

"And that was the way for my dad to show us what it was going to take, and that there's no excuses. It doesn't matter what your background is. If you have a desire to accomplish something, you'll find a way. Hard work comes in all different forms and circumstances. If you have a desire to make it, you'll make it happen."

He would need that desire. Five times between 2007 and 2011 Tony tried—and failed—to pass golf-qualifying school. In his sixth attempt, in 2013, he broke through, earning his tour card on the Web.com Tour, the equivalent of AAA baseball to the PGA Tour's major leagues. That meant he was one step—albeit a giant one—from the big time. Then, following a victory in a 2013 Web.com Tour stop in California, Finau officially became a member of the PGA Tour.

"It was a feeling of validation and unfinished business," Tony said. "You did it. Now what?"

And four years after he debuted, here he was down the road a piece from Augusta National, at Augusta Country Club, seated with me in the bar area discussing the journey—just three miles and three weeks from teeing off at the epicenter of golf's big time—the Masters.

The previous day he'd driven down the iconic Magnolia Lane, which leads from Augusta's Washington Road, down a perfectly paved drive and underneath a canopy of impeccably manicured oak trees to the Augusta National clubhouse, before which rests a burst of yellow marigold flowers, planted in the shape of the Masters logo. It is among the most iconic in sports. And it was something Finau had seen only on television and in his dreams. It surpassed every expectation. It made him emotional.

"With everything I've been through in my personal and professional life, it was very surreal, like an out-of-body experience," he said. "It's indescribable. I thought about my parents a lot, and being a little kid with big dreams.

"I watched the Masters for the first time in 1997, when Tiger won, and it inspired me to become a professional golfer. If Tiger didn't do that in '97, I'd probably be playing basketball somewhere, maybe overseas, maybe in the NBA, who knows, but I'd be playing basketball somewhere. He drove my attention to the game of golf because of what he did in the 1997 Masters."

I broached the journey with Kelepi in an unexpected and unorthodox setting: the pro shop at Augusta National on Masters Sunday, 2018. The final round was under way, and we were both thumbing through racks of leftover oversized quarter-zip pullover sweatshirts when Kelepi introduced himself to me. He is a jolly man, indescribably proud of his son. He should be. Throughout our conversation, he often flashed the same smile Tony inherited.

Kelepi said hello—he recognized my hair—and told me he appreciated the attention ESPN had given to Tony during our Masters coverage. That coverage wasn't forced. For the first several days of the tournament, Tony *was* the story. On Wednesday of Masters week, during the annual Par 3 Contest, Finau hit a hole-in-one on the seventh, leaped jubilantly in celebration, and backpedaled down the fairway like a football defensive back.

He was living a childhood dream. Cue the nightmare.

Suddenly, his left foot contorted awkwardly and his ankle rolled outward and dislocated—in front of millions of viewers.

The thought of it makes me cringe. Finau's immediate reaction was to reach down, grab his ankle, and jam it right back into place. And that's what he did. He spontaneously refused to entertain the thought of exiting the course on a stretcher after such a landmark personal moment. And then he finished the tournament.

Just before Finau's injury occurred, I had packed up my belongings to leave the course. My phone rang. I was the one guy at ESPN who knew him. So my bosses summoned me to the ninth green to await his exit from the Par 3 course to gauge his thoughts on how the injury might impact his Masters debut. As he gingerly walked up the hill toward a golf cart he smiled and we hugged, and I asked him if he was all right. He was on the way to see his doctor to find out.

He smiled that smile in an attempt to mask the concern in his eyes. It didn't work. In twelve hours he was slated to achieve everything he'd ever dreamed of and worked for as a golfer. He would tee off at the Masters. And now it might not happen. As he climbed the hill to learn his fate, he again found perspective in the journey.

"I've been through worse, Marty," he told me, sitting in that golf cart. "If I can play without hurting it worse, I'll play. I'll text you what I find out."

Off he went. I could sense his heartbreak just then. But I knew exactly what he meant.

Weeks before during our previous conversation, Finau explained to me why he always wears green shirts on Sunday final rounds. Green was his mother's favorite color, and he wears it to remember her.

On November 27, 2011, at four o'clock in the morning, Tony and his siblings awoke to news that their mother, brother, and sister were involved in a tragic car accident while driving home from a wedding in Reno. Tony and his family convened in his aunt's living room, held hands, and sang a church hymn before driving to the accident site in Nevada. Midway there, Kelepi received a call.

He immediately pulled the car over and began vomiting and sobbing uncontrollably.

Ravena, his wife of twenty-six years, had died.

"She was the rock," Tony said. "It was tough on our family. Every word that *mom* means, she was to our family. She loved us and took care of us, and she was always there for me."

Less than twenty-four hours later, Tony became a father. His first child, a son, was born.

Finau suddenly had a piercing perspective on the circle of life.

"I felt like there was new life for me instantly," Finau said. "I took on this role as Dad, and I went through a rough stretch of five or six months trying to understand my purpose. Was it to continue to play? How am I going to provide for my son? And the decision of my girlfriend at the time—is she the right one to be married to? There was a lot going on in my life."

He worried so much he developed a debilitating ulcer. For five weeks he could not walk. For eight, he couldn't play golf.

"It changed my perspective on life," he continued. "I had to grow up really fast. When you have a son to take care of, and you're thinking about another person outside of yourself, your purpose in life becomes a little stronger, and your desire to become somebody or be somebody, because there's another kid that's going to be looking up to you who's your responsibility, I had to mature fast.

"I feel like I was a pretty mature kid, but turning yourself from a kid to a dad is a life-changing moment."

And he said that day defined his purpose. I wondered what he believed his purpose to be.

"I feel like my responsibility is that anybody who comes into contact with me, that there's a light," he explained. "You have to shine and be bright, and be a light to those around you. I definitely think that's my only purpose—to be a light around anybody I come into contact with.

"And if they understand where that light and that source comes from, then I've done my job. As much as I want to be a great golfer and accomplish things in golf—and those are all great things—I do think I have a bigger and stronger purpose, and that's to be a light to everyone I meet."

To whom much is given, from him much is expected. For the first time ever, someone had articulated my exact feelings. Work hard. Be kind. Tony Finau defined my purpose right before me and directly to me.

I stopped the interview. I wonder often in thought or prayer, sometimes aloud all by myself, why God gave me this life. Why did He choose me to meet these inspiring people who are heroes to so many? Why did He choose me to fellowship with them? To learn from them? To spend intimate time with them? What did I do to deserve that and what does He want from me in return?

Be a light. Be so full of joy and enthusiasm and appreciation and kindness that everyone in your midst feels it and cannot deny it. I will forever be inspired by that moment. And I will try my hardest to be a better version of myself tomorrow than I am today. I won't always succeed. I'm not always full of appreciation or kindness. I lose my way sometimes, whether due to ego or insecurity or pride.

But I try to live my life the way Finau described he's living his: Be kind; work hard. The rest takes care of itself.

i love you, L

Small gestures requiring minimal effort can have massive impact.

With a simple smile, a hello, or a handwritten thank-you card, you can change the course of an entire day. Immediately the world is better. You may roll your eyes at that sentiment, consider it hokey, but it's true. You can make the world better without much work.

I am a staunch advocate of handwritten letters. I write them to everybody. If I've interviewed someone in the past decade, they most likely received a handwritten thank-you letter from me. This is undeniable: The two minutes it requires to write, seal, stamp, and send a handwritten note to someone who did something kind for you, believed in you, or gave you time or insight or a thoughtful gift, will buy you a lifetime in that person's heart.

Trust me on this. It is gospel.

And the power of a simple question is mighty. We've all experienced that moment when someone inquired about our day, and instantly our day improved and took on a positive direction. Sometimes in this life we just want acknowledgment—especially as our world shifts further and further away from human interaction, and closer and closer to what I like to call "device-olation."

We live in our phones: eyes down, nose up, posture lazy, interactions intangible and devoid of inflection or body language, attention stolen, reality skewed. Facebook? More like Fake Book. Like most parents, Lainie and I aren't especially sure how to achieve balance between the world that mobile devices open and the world they close.

It saddens me. I say often how badly I wish my children could grow up the way I grew up—which both my parents said to my sister and me ad nauseam.

I met Lainie at a fraternity party while in college at Radford (Virginia) University. It was January 10, 1997. We were buddies for months before we became a couple. (More on that later in the book.) Early in our friendship, she began making mixtapes for me, which included songs she liked or that moved her emotionally, and which she wrapped in intricate self-produced cover art that spoke to her consideration of me as a human being and a friend.

One had a middle finger in the air. I never asked why. Another was an intricate clover she drew, and yet another was a series of numeral 9s—my favorite number. One simply stated, "Bird Meat," which she once said while we were drinking, and I laughed hysterically at the way it sounded leaving her lips. I made her say it over and over again, and I laughed harder and harder.

More than twenty years have passed. We still howl at bird meat.

Those mixtapes made me feel really special. They were the manifestation of time she spent thinking of me. Their sole purpose was to connect us. As couples mature together, those efforts to remain connected can wane, and for most of us they almost always do. It takes effort to make your spouse of many years feel important and special and wonderful.

But not much effort.

I think about my failures a lot. Every day I consider the man I am, and the man I want to be for Lainie and our children. And when I fail, which is often, I recall a two-sentence letter Lainie wrote me in black Sharpie on some leftover stationery she found from my first day at NASCAR, May 3, 1999. The notepad is pocket-sized and has my name printed on it in navy blue, alongside the official NASCAR logo.

Have fun on the radio.

i love you,

L.

The *i* is lowercase. The *L* is a beautiful swooping and swirling cursive mark, shorthand for her legal signature.

And I don't know why, but those two sentences, which were an unexpected surprise resting on my computer keyboard when I awoke early one Saturday morning for the ESPN Radio program *Marty & McGee*, said so much more to me than "Have fun" and "I love you."

They told me she believes in me, and that the man I am is the man she needs, despite my failures and flaws, and that she appreciates the grind.

Ultimately, it means she thought of me.

It was a married-couple mixtape.

Chapter Nineteen

Always Dreaming

Two days before the 2018 Kentucky Derby, on a nervous Thursday morning at dawn, I walked into the barn stable area at Churchill Downs in Louisville, Kentucky, horse racing's most treasured venue, home to the twin spires and the world's most cherished race, the Derby.

The barns at Churchill are pristine, white with green roofs, and each of the superstar trainers has his own, specific barn for the fleet of horses he seeks to make champions. At this moment I knew nothing. I knew no one. It was like being dropped into a foreign land, ignorant to customs or laws and incapable of speaking the language. You have to learn rather quickly using context clues and perceptions.

I just stood there, lost, looking around like a doofus, wondering how I might negotiate this new world.

The sun sparkled through the trees and into the courtyard before me. Training assistants bathed horses, fresh from predawn galloping, their rippling muscles glistening in the sunlight. They are beautiful athletes, massive and lean and confident.

As I watched, I felt rather certain that no one on these hallowed grounds was more ignorant about the nuances of horse racing than me. That is not hyperbole. I knew so little I feared embarrassment. Horse racing is like NASCAR: If you don't speak the language and know how to move confidently within the arena, you're a fraud. And like NASCAR, these folks have a staunch, distinct pride for their life's passion that doesn't suffer frauds well.

Nor should they.

I didn't know it yet, but I had two very important things going for me: I had an experienced, well-educated producer named Kristine Kugler, an ESPN veteran of countless events, who knew everyone in the paddock and the sport's history, to hold my hand.

And I had college football. God bless college football.

As I stood there, outside one of those white-and-green barns, staring blankly while attempting not to look like I was staring blankly, trying to process the challenge before me, a handsome gentleman with white hair tucked under a ball cap walked out of an office and said hello, in unique fashion.

"Hey! *College GameDay*! What are you doing here?"

I looked around. He was talking to me.

"I haven't one damn clue."

He liked that answer, and we shared a good laugh. It eased my anxiety. I figured we'd get along all right. I noticed instantly he was wearing a University of Arizona zip-up jacket. (I would later learn that Arizona is like horse-racing Harvard.)

He inquired about my thoughts on Kevin Sumlin, the football coach who'd recently been fired from Texas A&M and subsequently hired at UA.

I adore Kevin Sumlin, and I instantly said as much. I felt like Sumlin's personality was more befitting Tucson than it was College Station, and that his preexisting recruiting penetration of talent-rich Phoenix and Scottsdale would be crucial to his success in rebuilding Arizona. With time and patience, I felt that he would do well.

Turns out, after this minutes-long dissertation, the guy was friends with Sumlin. Thank God I didn't trash him. After maybe ten minutes of ball talk, I realized I hadn't even introduced myself. Embarrassed, I finally did so. And then I asked the gentleman what his role was around the stable.

He looked at me quizzically, smiled, shifted his body weight toward the barn, pointed over his shoulder, and said the most mortifying thing I could possibly imagine: "See those horses? I train 'em. C'mon. I'll introduce you."

The gentleman was Todd Pletcher, he of multiple Kentucky Derby championships fame, he who had trained Always Dreaming to the Derby crown just *one year before*. I was absolutely mortified, embarrassed, and annoyingly apologetic.

I tried to stifle my embarrassment. But the red in my cheeks shone through the red in my beard. I felt like such an idiot. In that moment I was everything I'd hoped to avoid. And I'd just gotten started.

Pletcher loved it.

He was so accustomed to having his ass kissed, he appreciated the opportunity to teach a novice. And I was more than willing to learn. Opportunities like that are a reporter's currency. Opportunities like that enable a reporter to paint a picture for the viewer or the reader. It's difficult to describe the value of simply being able to say, "I spoke to Todd Pletcher, who led Always Dreaming to the Kentucky Derby championship last year..." But trust me, it's valuable.

He took me into the barn and introduced me to his horses, including Always Dreaming. Then he dug into the pocket of his soiled jeans and handed me one of those star mints, like the ones you grab at the welcome desk when exiting a restaurant, and he showed me how to hold out my hand, open and flat with the mint in the middle, and the horse would slurp it right out of my hand. And so I did.

And here I was, in this green barn with this legendary trainer, and his championship steed, worth notably more than my home, ate a restaurant mint right out of my hand and left its valuable snot and slobber behind.

And Pletcher immediately grabbed my hand and shook it.

It was quite a moment of blissful ignorance.

"Innocence"

The wonder in my daughters' eyes is beautiful and mysterious. There are times when all is quiet and they're staring off into nothingness, straight-faced and carefree, worriless, and I yearn to know what's walking through those precious little minds. Whatever that answer may be is the "X" on a parent's buried treasure map. If we could unlock it, riches of innocence beyond measure would spill out. I sit and watch them sometimes when they play together. The air is a chorus of brilliant ideas and laughter, pretend brought to life. And I think about them as adults and how terribly I'll miss these times when they're small. It makes me emotional. One day I tried to put those feelings to paper.

Innocence

Sippin' on Jack 'n' water...
Starin' at my daughter...
Thinkin' 'bout all the fodder...
That troubles my soul...

She's an angel with a crayon...
She just wants to play on...

Ain't worried about the payoff...
The dollar or the day off...
In a world that takes a toll...

I hope to teach her through my action...
That life, when filled with passion...
Is focus amid distraction...
Is peace and love and satisfaction...
In a world she can't control.

Chapter Twenty

Boston. Stronger.

Few emotional outlets unify us the way sports do. Even when we're divided by allegiance, we're bonded by experience. Games aren't church, but they do spiritually inspire us and provide a passionate community for individuals with similar beliefs to convene and fellowship. And in some cases, to worship.

And like Sunday service, sports have distinct healing power.

On April 21, 2014, that healing power was unmistakable as I walked to the starting line for the 118th running of the Boston Marathon. It was unseasonably warm at race time, a nice relief from a long, cold winter. And for this proud region that for a year had felt shackled by grief and loss, it was another reason to rejoice.

This wasn't just race day. This was resurrection day. The air that morning was crisp, the sun brilliant. It felt free. The streets were packed with people, a million of them, several rows deep from the street, standing and cheering and living, purging a year of hurt and celebrating a rebirth and an uprising against cowardice and terror.

Marathon Monday always falls on Patriots' Day. Their day. And no evil would stop them from the joy it instills. For most of us outside of New England, Patriots' Day is just another Monday. It's an unwelcome alarm clock and the anxiety of predawn traffic and a relentless barrage of deadlines to meet. But in New England, Patriots' Day is the best day.

It is First Beer at 9 and First Wave at 10 and First Pitch at 11.

It is passion and it is tradition and it is belonging, a bond that links families and strangers and generations of both. And those brothers with those bombs tried to strip it. They wounded Boston. But like a broken bone, with time Boston healed stronger.

On April 15, 2013, like so many of you, I sat on my couch transfixed on the television as the horrific aftermath of the marathon bombing unfolded. It was quite literally chaos in the streets. Lives were lost and forever altered. Innocence was robbed. It pissed me off. Those cowards stuffed backpacks full of pressure cookers containing explosives with the intention of hurting innocent people.

Meanwhile, I was communicating with a producer friend of mine, Andrea Pelkey, with whom I'd worked closely at ESPN for years on the auto racing beat. She lived in Boston's Back Bay neighborhood, a proud New Englander from birth, a Maine girl, tough and smart and independent. She was very scared and very sad. We told each other we'd train and we'd run and we'd hold each other accountable and, ultimately, in that minute sliver of a way, we'd help heal through participation and spirit. We would run as a tribute to those who couldn't.

I trained my ass off, diligently, for months, pushed my body with neurotic consistency through cutting wind in Philadelphia and driving rain in Phoenix and icy snow in Charlotte and Miami humidity so thick it felt like I was breathing through plastic wrap. I quit drinking alcohol almost completely, trading the morning fog for the morning dew, swapping fun for fuel. Most days I ate more than six thousand calories.

I ran nearly every day. I ran ten miles on Thanksgiving and

thirteen miles on Christmas and fourteen miles on New Year's Day. Stick to the schedule. Do not waver. Puke and rally. Two miles from home on a long run in February, I lost concentration for the briefest moment. I paid for it. It was a lesson. The individual concrete slabs that combine to make up the sidewalk on Washam Potts Road in Cornelius, North Carolina, do not rest flush against one another. The slabs had settled into the soil at different heights. And when I lost focus deep into the run, my toe failed to clear a higher-resting slab on the downswing of my gait.

I stubbed my toe. And I went ass-over-teakettle, a complete yard sale.

The first thing that hit the sidewalk was my left shoulder and the side of my head. The next thing that hit was my right hand, in which I clutched my iPhone. My head split open and my phone shattered. A pair of ladies in a forest green Ford minivan drove up, stopped, and asked if I was injured. I told them I was not. I was fine, just embarrassed. I lay there for several moments to make sure I wasn't lying to them.

My longest training run was twenty-two miles. It was miserable. It took about three hours and fifteen minutes and included every type of terrain—pavement, gravel, winding dirt trails, and a lot of hills. When I left my home I could see my breath. A few miles in, the sky opened. So for eighteen-plus miles, I ran in forty-degree rain. It kept on and I kept on. I figured if my body could withstand that brand of misery, and the chafing and the blisters that came with it, there wasn't much Boston could throw at me that I couldn't handle.

Endurance sports challenge me mentally as much as they do physically. Racing the clock every day can leave you feeling unprepared. During training my mind is always racing, even in bed. I constantly extrapolate my pace to equate it to 26.2 miles. I had to beat four hours. As far as I was concerned, failing to do so meant failing altogether.

For me, the mental aspect of running is both liberating and debilitating. If you let doubt creep in, you're done. So always demand much of yourself while training.

Because of that effort and the perspective it offers, I developed a thought process about running, honed during those hours of solitude and reflection on the pavement and the dirt: The road looks different to the man who has walked it.

It sounds simple. It's not. And it equates to sport and to life.

Our opinions of others' reactions or decisions might not be favorable. But we don't have the right to judge, because we don't often have proper context on what variables produced those reactions or decisions. Life is a journey. Life is a road. And unless you walk that road, you don't know its quirks and fissures and tendencies and divots and blemishes and hills and valleys. No road can be fully respected in a car. Its character and holes and patches and wind and elements are all generally anonymous in a car.

But not to a runner.

The runner bears it all. What is flat to a rider can be Everest to a runner. A beautiful day in a car can be harsh to a runner. The road looks different to the man who has walked it.

Boston looks different now. Because I walked it. Because I ran it.

I was anxious on Marathon Monday. I didn't feel prepared. Boston is a point-to-point marathon. You start in one town and finish 26.2 miles away in another town. Other marathons I've run are more cyclical. You finish where you start.

In Boston, you take a school bus from Boston Common out to Hopkinton. It's a thirty-mile drive west on Interstate 90. At 45 miles per hour, it takes a while, and most runners hydrate throughout the morning to defend against cramping later. It was warmer than normal on Marathon Monday in 2014, and many runners, even elite ones, miscalculated hydration and electrolyte balance. I certainly miscalculated.

Halfway down the highway to Hopkinton, a group of us on that bus had to pee really badly. The bus driver pulled over, and about ten of us scurried down the aisle and out of the bus, up an embankment into a wooded area, hopscotching through roadside trash, chose a tree, and let it fly. So there I was, on the side of the highway in suburban Boston, privates in hand, and I look up to see a family having breakfast through the large kitchen window in the back of their home. I'm uncertain if they were looking out. If so, they got a show. I quickly spun around, stream flowing, directly into a wind gust. I peed on myself before I ever got started. Unreal.

When we arrived they grouped us in a field with our respective waves, which is running lingo for starting-time groupings. Random sweatshirts and hats and pairs of sweatpants littered the field. As runners' waves are called to the starting line, they shed layers of warmth for the freedom of speed.

As I walked to the starting line I passed a group of twenty-somethings in front of a small white house, carrying a basketful of "race essentials." They were handing out Marlboro Menthols and Bud Light. From there I continued on into a massive herd of humanity. The air was anxious as folks prepared for the gun blast that would signal the start for their wave and the manifestation of months of preparation, as this rowdy block party in Hopkinton blended into Framingham, and then into Natick and Wellesley and Brookline and Newton, and then on to Boston, a twenty-seven-mile celebration of the region and the runners and the rebirth.

Because, to paraphrase Red Sox legend David Ortiz, it's their f——ing city.

Never before had their city been prouder than on this day. Not even when their Sox or their Celtics or their Bruins or their Patriots won world championships. Not ever. This was about more than pride. This was about closure.

They had already rallied. For an entire year, Boston had bonded together in support of those injured and killed in the marathon bombings. But this was the anniversary of the event. This was the ultimate display of Boston Strong. And I still can't believe I was a participant.

I was a participant due only to charity. Unlike many of the great runners here, I did not earn my way into the race with a great performance in a qualifying event. I was thirty-eight years old the year I ran. The required finishing time for a thirty-eight-year-old male is three hours, ten minutes. That is absolutely flying. I am not that fast. So, like many others, I went the charity route for entrance.

I ran on behalf of Tenacity, a literacy-based nonprofit benefiting underserved youth in Boston, which uses books and tennis to keep kids' minds fresh and their bodies fit. It does wonderful things. *Perfect*, I thought. *I'm a writer. I work for ESPN. It's a great match.* Tenacity accepted me, and twenty others, onto the team. Together, we raised $180,000 for the kids in Boston.

The race was difficult. Managing emotion was a chore. I openly wept three times. Ugly crying is not conducive to great athletic performance. The first was somewhere around mile 7. I was cruising at this point—an 8-minute-per-mile pace—although, for reasons I still can't pinpoint, my heart rate was entirely too high. During training, I averaged around 145 beats per minute. At that time, I was in the 160s. Maybe it was the emotion. Maybe it was the antibiotic I was taking for a sinus infection. Whatever it was, it would haunt me later.

A girl named Kaitlyn, decked out in neon yellow, flanked me to my left. Like most folks around me, she was running for charity. Suddenly a group of spectators to our right erupted in cheers, screaming her name. She darted directly in front of me to embrace them. It was wonderful to witness. I got choked up about it, but said out loud to myself to let that go. If I was to finish the race, I couldn't let those moments affect me. I would see them all day. I would need to remind myself of this more than once.

An amazing moment for every marathoner is finding family and friends along the course. It is a jolt of energy and clarity, a reminder of why you made the decision to participate. Lainie and our friend Greg Morin, at the time the pit crew coach for Jimmie Johnson's and Dale Earnhardt Jr.'s NASCAR teams at Hendrick Motorsports, came to support me. Their experience was a comedy of errors, the first of which came at mile 10.

They took a fifty-dollar cab ride from Boston to Natick and meandered their way through backyards and over fences to the course. It was at that time that they received a text message update about my progress. According to the data, I was right beside them. Lainie turned around and there I was, cruising. I pointed in their direction, ran directly toward them, and high-fived the nine-year-old standing ten feet from them. I never saw them.

The signs along the course were poignant and proud and hilarious:

> Chuck Norris Never Ran a Marathon!
> Go Nads!
> Today Is the Only Day It's Okay to Poop Your Pants.

I followed one guy for probably a mile. Then I looked up and realized his shirt read, in black Sharpie, "Sorry, I farted." I passed him before he could pass gas. My favorite, on an orange poster board held high in the air by a young girl and written in Sharpie in black, block capital letters: "THIS IS OUR F——ING CITY."

In Framingham, I eased up a hill toward a left-hand curve. There was a group of twenty-somethings perched on a roof. Blinking behind them was one of those road-construction warning signs, only there was no warning. There was a statement that read, in orange letters: "Boston, One Year Stronger." That got me. The folks in Framingham were loud. It was awesome. The streets were electric.

Somewhere thereabouts, a young lady stood atop a perch alongside the road, furiously waving an American flag with all her might, screaming as loudly as she could: *"An American won the Boston Marathon!!!!"* It was Meb Keflezighi. Every single runner, all of us, cheered and clapped. We were participants in the first Boston Marathon won by an American runner since 1983. What an honor.

One of the most moving moments for me was meeting Dick and Rick Hoyt, the father-son duo who had ran more than thirty Boston Marathons together. The 2014 edition marked their thirty-second. Rick, then fifty-two, has cerebral palsy. Dick, then seventy-three, pushed him in a custom jogging stroller. I was running along and saw a group of five or six folks, decked out in red Team Hoyt shirts, surrounding a stroller in a semicircle formation. I had no idea about their story. But everyone lining the streets was losing their minds for these guys. I was moved. I ran over, grabbed Rick by the arm, pumped my fist in the air, and told him he was a badass. Because he's a badass.

I got weepy in that moment, too. If you have a soul, seeing that moves you.

Per tradition, I kissed a girl in Wellesley near mile 13. Her sign read "Kiss Me I'm from Miami Beach!" That was good enough for me. I ran over to the far right of what is known as the Scream Tunnel—a sea of Wellesley College students whose classes are canceled for the day—and smooched her cheek. Yikes. She was half my age.

The crowd's passion is a towrope of emotion. It pulls you when you believe you can't go farther. I wanted to quit at mile 17. The tinge of cramping began just then, and I knew I was in trouble. I pulled over to the side and clutched my right hamstring. It felt as if there were a baseball embedded beneath my skin. I tried to massage it out and reached down to stretch it. As I extended my leg, my quadriceps seized up. I was more than nine miles from the finish line, and my entire right leg was locked in a cramp.

This perplexed me. I felt that I had hydrated well, prepared my body well through grueling distance runs in Daytona and Phoenix and Las Vegas and all over Charlotte. I felt that my nutrition was right.

At that point, fear set in, the concern that I wouldn't finish what I'd started, the self-doubt that all of my goals might now be impossible. *No. I won't let them be impossible. I will not lose.* I decided to worry about potential injury later. Today I would manage the pain as best I could, pound Gatorade at every fluid station, and simply work through it.

I would finish, damn it, even if it meant crawling home at midnight. This was bigger than any pain could suppress.

I managed to run through it, verbally prodding myself to put one foot in front of the next. But it hurt. (I would find out later over a few post-race Sam Adams beers that even some elite runners battled cramping that day. They get paid to know how to eat and drink.)

Newton brought more doubt. The Newton Hills are a series of middle fingers. You'll be running along on what, by comparison, is a flat plane, and as far up as you can see to the horizon line there are runners. Thousands of them. Bright dots of color bouncing along. And all you can think is, *Damn it. I have to run up that thing.*

The last of the Newton Hills is Heartbreak. Heartbreak Hill is aptly named. After I missed Lainie and Greg at mile 10, they jumped back in a cab and went to the top of Heartbreak, where they waited for me. They stationed themselves by the stoplight atop the hill, on the left side of the road, so I wouldn't miss them again, then texted me their whereabouts. I ran with my phone in order to communicate with Lainie, listen to music, and document the journey.

Siri doesn't understand country accents well.

When that stoplight came into view, I dug deep. I had the best-laid plan: Get to the top, embrace my wife and friend, snap some photographs, and chat a moment. When I reached them, I fell into Lainie, mumbled, "My God, this is so hard," and then took off. I singsonged in my head like Dory from *Finding Nemo*: *Just keep running*. Again, they were disappointed.

I had to walk at times in the final stages. At mile 23, I physically pushed a spectator away from the gate so I could stretch my right calf. I wasn't being rude. At that point, it's about maintaining movement. There is no shame. Snot rockets and loogies are shot and spit. Folks crap their pants and just keep running. Some runners lock up completely, fall over, get back up, and slug it home.

It's Boston. The most prestigious marathon on earth. You do whatever it takes to earn that medal. I ran the final three miles virtually straightlegged. If I bent my knees, my quads or hamstrings would fire back up.

As I entered the city, I thought instantly about 2013. The famous Citgo sign outside Fenway Park came into view. I knew I was getting close. I ran down a hill and under a tunnel with a sign that read "1K to Go." I tried like hell to do the math. I couldn't.

I strode on until I reached the final left turn of the race, at Boylston Street. Four blocks from glory. Four blocks from where that bomb exploded 371 days before. When I took that left, it felt like the seas parted. The street got very wide and the crowd very vocal, as if it was their mission to guide us home. I expected the finish line to be very close once I took that left. It wasn't. Well into distance runs, my eyes tend to get foggy.

The closer I got to the finish line, the clearer the timing clock got. It said 3:58:something. I freaked out. Any time greater than four hours, to me, was an unacceptable effort, given the training it took to get there. So I tried to sprint. My legs were a mess. I managed to get my left knee bent enough to run faster. At this point, I was at a ten-plus-minute pace.

I made it. As I crossed the line, the clock read 3:59:07. I can't articulate the feeling in my legs. I'd run marathons before. But this was harder. All I wanted to do was sit down, but I knew if I didn't keep walking, the entire lower half of my body would lock up. So I walked. And as I walked, I heard my name.

I looked to my right, and there stood Boston police officer Brian Smigielski. My friend. He ran over to me. I didn't look too good. He wanted to put me in a wheelchair, but I'm hardheaded. I wouldn't have it. I was there for Sean Collier, the MIT police officer who was slain by the bombers. Sean's brother, Andy, was my friend and he is Greg's friend. I also ran for Chase Kowalski, the sweet little seven-year-old boy who was murdered at Sandy Hook, and who loved to run. His parents, Rebecca and Steve, host triathlons in his memory.

I was there to run for those who couldn't, and now I could damn sure walk for them.

But as we walked I cramped badly, so I sat on the curb to stretch. But all I could do was put my head between my knees and cry. I still don't know why.

Smigielski—"Smig," as we call him—put his hands on my shoulders. He didn't know what to say to me. Finally a doctor came by and suggested that I should stand and move or I'd be in worse shape quickly. Lainie and Greg were several blocks down at Arlington Street. They couldn't get any closer because of the security measures in place as a result of the previous year's tragedy. So I had to walk to them.

Smig helped me up, then looked at one of his brothers and barked, "Man this post. I'm taking my friend to his family."

I cry every time I think about that. He will never know what he did for me just then. Someday I hope I can explain that to him.

As I hobbled down Boylston Street, a new respect washed over me for the runners in the 2013 Boston Marathon who had felt just the way I felt right then, but who had the resolve and the humanity to console the injured, to tear off their shirts and manufacture tourniquets. To save lives and limbs. To run toward the fire.

The Boston Marathon is a spiritual experience that creates community and belonging, along with a painful euphoria. I will never view it the same way.

The road looks different to the man who has walked it.

Chapter Twenty-One

Wally World

Lainie and I were not instant lovebirds.

She's a South Jersey beach girl, born and raised in Ocean City just around the corner from the water, so the man of her dreams looked like Kelly Slater or the Ocean City Beach Patrol North Street lifeguards, buff and bronzed and fit. The man of her dreams did not look like Chip Hackler from *Shag*. No sir, a pale, skinny, freckled, pimpled ginger, with an uneven self-clipped buzz cut and an Appalachian accent, raised working on a cattle farm, was not her plan.

We met in the fire code disaster that is a basement fraternity party. It was packed and dank and deafening. It smelled like beer and mold. Nineties hits like Luniz's "I Got 5 on It" and Ginuwine's "Pony" and DJ Kool's "Let Me Clear My Throat" and Keith Sweat's "Twisted" were very popular. Those songs played on a loop at every party and in the one dance club in town, called Riverview.

I recall meeting Lainie at the Delta Chi fraternity house. She remembers our location as a place called Detox. Regardless, it wasn't necessarily happenstance. Lainie's roommate, Beth, had a big crush on my buddy from back home. He was on the Radford

University basketball team and had droopy eyes. They lived in the same dormitory, Tyler Hall, which had the nicest computer lab on the RU campus, maybe five rows of six bulky white Macintosh desktop machines. At the time, this room was state of the art, the stuff college brochures are written about.

We didn't have our own laptops back then. So when it came time to write essays or research papers we posted up in that computer lab—for hours. That required patience and planning. Rare was the day you simply walked in and sat down. Typically you waited until another student completed his or her task and left the room. If Lainie and Beth walked by and peeked inside, and Bryan was using that computer lab, they'd walk in and "check email." She'd had her eye on him for a while.

So when Lainie and her other girlfriend mustered up enough liquid courage at the fraternity soiree, they shoved Beth into my friend. Beth was cute and bubbly and hilarious. My buddy was figuring out life. Off they went.

Lainie and her friend couldn't stop giggling about the fact that they'd shoved Beth into Bryan. I stood there, unsure what to do. Lainie said she recognized me.

"You're the guy from Quest, right!"

Quest is Radford lingo for freshman orientation.

I was not the guy from Quest.

We went our separate ways.

The cool kids were milling about the party, raising many brands of hell. Lainie and I weren't cool. I was easily embarrassed back then, so I found a corner and held up the wall like Poindexter, underneath some stairs, clutching a Milwaukee's Best Light and doing my very best to pretend to enjoy it. Lainie was over in another corner with another friend, also hiding. I wasn't good at approaching people in those days. It gave me a lot of anxiety. But eventually I was bored and buzzed enough to walk back over there.

Lainie was sipping cinnamon liquor from a Lion King kiddie cup. I asked her to dance. I don't dance. I later learned she agreed out of something close to pity, I assume from the anxiety welling in my eyes with the fear of rejection. Some people are unaffected by rejection. I am not one of those people. I am greatly affected. Lainie agreed, but demanded her friend not leave her. It was girl code for "Get this dude away from me."

Her friend left her.

We enjoyed the evening and began to notice each other more often. Before then we were in similar circles but had paid each other no mind.

With time we grew to really enjoy hanging out together. We made each other laugh and think. I would stop by her dorm room nearly every day just to see her. If I didn't, my day felt incomplete. One of those days was move-out day her sophomore year. Her father was there packing up her belongings. I walked into a roomful of people and said hello to everyone there. That's how I was taught. Her father wasn't impressed. He didn't appreciate my oversized basketball shorts and thought I was a punk. He was right.

Lainie supported me at Radford basketball games, about which she couldn't have cared less. I was a student volunteer in the sports communications group, and tabulated statistics of games while wearing some oversized pleated jeans and a brown corduroy vest wrestled over a triple-extra-large white T-shirt. What a mess. We just enjoyed each other.

Which leads us to the time early in our friendship when I asked her to join me on an outing.

Growing up in the country, my friends and I found unique ways to entertain ourselves. This was pre-iPhone, so if we wanted to talk to our buddies, we had to get up off our butts and walk to their house, or at the very least pick up the telephone and rotary-dial the house phone number. (If you were lucky or wealthy, you had the extra-long cord that enabled you a unique mobility—you could drag the phone into another room for privacy.) That meant we actually had to address the parents, and politely request to chat with their daughter or son. Text messages and social media didn't exist.

Thank God they didn't exist. If they had, this book probably wouldn't.

Anyway, we did some really dumb crap for entertainment. An example: When we were kids in Pearisburg, my buddies and I would go to the Magic Mart department store in town and buy those inflatable rafts, the ones that included the blue plastic oars. We'd discard the raft, grab a hacksaw, and cut the two oars into four bazookas.

We'd take the four plastic tubes, stuff our pockets with sleeves of bottle-rocket fireworks, and grab the random Bic lighter from Daddy's sock drawer; then we'd stage us a neighborhood bottle-rocket war.

It went like this: Shove a rocket into the bazooka, lay it up on your shoulder, light it, and watch your buddies run like hell. Our youthful invincibility made the scene hilarious. If you're thinking that's the stupidest thing you've ever read, well, you are correct. I cannot believe we actually did that. If my kids did that today, I'd feel like a parental failure. But we did it—until I took one in the side of the neck that damn near blew my ear off. That ended the bottle-rocket war action real quick. I thought my mother was going to disown me.

Another keen activity was lighting random items on fire and shooting them with a .22 rifle. My best friend growing up was Mark Vinson. As I've mentioned, we are still very close and correspond almost daily. He grew up to work professionally in sports as well, as a member of the Tampa Bay Rays athletic training staff. As kids we watched a lot of midsummer 3 p.m. Atlanta Braves games on television. Dale Murphy and Rafael Ramirez and Bruce Sutter and Bob Horner. Those Braves.

Eventually we'd get bored and decide to go shoot things. We'd grab random items like G.I. Joe figurines or plastic model F-16 airplanes, take them out back, hose them down with some lighter fluid, and set them on fire. Then, for good measure, we'd load up a .22 and start blasting away until nothing was left but tiny smoldering charred particles of plastic.

I mean, what the hell?

These days kids would be cuffed and stuffed. In 1987 in Pearisburg, Virginia, that was a Saturday afternoon.

When we got a bit older and could drive, we traded the Braves for girls. And girls meant the mall.

New River Valley Mall was thirty miles away in Christiansburg, and Valley View Mall was sixty miles away in Roanoke. Roanoke was like Manhattan for us. The Star City. The big city. Like many teens, we barely had any money, so we'd get an Orange Julius smoothie or a small TCBY sundae and just walk around the mall looking at girls. Eventually, we'd head over to the Walmart to mess around and look at pocket knives and flashlights and firearms.

This is where Lainie comes in. Several months into our friendship but before we started dating, we were hanging out every day. So when my buddy Foster called and said he was headed to Walmart and invited Lainie and me to join him and his girlfriend, I thought nothing of it. Hell yeah we will.

I called Lainie.

"What are you up to? Foster and I are headed over to the Wally World. You wanna come with us?"

At this point Lainie's feelings toward me had grown. She was excited and agreed to join us.

We stopped to pick her up and she walked out toward the car. This is college in the grunge era. Baggy clothes and sweats were the order of the day most of the time. The rest of us in the car wore sweatpants and T-shirts. And here Lainie came, dressed beautifully. Nice clothes. Makeup. Lipstick. She didn't often wear lipstick. Still doesn't. She jumped in and I was taken with how stunning she looked—and completely perplexed as to why she had dressed so well...to go to Walmart.

It wasn't until much later that she explained it to me.

She'd had a powwow briefing with her friends about what this mysterious "Wally World" actually was. They laid out several potential outfits based on the varying hypotheses. They settled on what they felt was the perfect getup.

When I said we were heading to Wally World, she thought we were going on a date. To Wally World. And she thought Wally World, as in the movie *National Lampoon's Vacation*...was an amusement park.

Somehow, I still won her.

Bomb Squad

Atlanta Braves Hall of Fame third baseman Chipper Jones was a founding member of a hunting group called Buck Commander, which grew to include other major leaguers, as well as celebrities like Duck Dynasty's Willie Robertson and country music stars Jason Aldean and Luke Bryan. Their antics included some legendary pranks. In my podcast, I asked Jones which moment he remembered most. It was, quite literally, a blast.

Adam LaRoche has a pretty good hunting spread out there in Kansas. And we were all in his little metal barn. Cement floor. He has a batting cage in there and a volleyball court, a real nice lounge and dinner area. He's got all his [hunting] mounts up on the wall. It's where he entertains. So Willie Robertson [of *Duck Dynasty*] and LaRoche's older brother, Jeff, were in this little prank war. And Jeff was a trooper—key word: was—out in Colorado. Willie took all of Jeff's clothes, put them in Jeff's suitcase, filled it full of water, and put it in the walk-in freezer. So that's what got all this started. So Jeff, thinking he was gonna be all cool and do the one-uppings, decides to throw a flash-bang. Willie is cooking dinner, okay? On a gas grill. Okay? And Jeff decides he's gonna throw a flash-bang up underneath Willie's legs and scare him. Metal building. Cement floor. Can you imagine what a flash-bang sounded like, man? I thought the world had ended. I thought somebody had discharged a weapon, somebody got shot, and everybody was diving for the couches. It was insane! Well, afterward Willie doesn't even know where he is, stumbles into the bathroom, and literally explodes the commode as he falls. The commode is in twelve different pieces. There's water everywhere. And I think Willie had a pretty serious knee injury from that incident. From that point, the monster pranks kind of ended. And I told [LaRoche], "Roachy, I love you. I love you like a play cousin, but you keep your brother away from me." That was inches from a gas grill. That whole place could've gone up!

Chapter Twenty-Two

Do as I Do

It was four o'clock in the morning at the South Rim entrance to the Grand Canyon. The Arizona sky was black, save for a matrix of bouncing headlamp beams piercing the darkness. Thick dust billowed in the air, rustled awake by our shuffling feet. That dust is always present here but rarely seen, emerging only when immersed in the light from headlamps.

With each breath, the dust rushed toward my nose and mouth and then ran away, like waves to the beach. I felt claustrophobic, even while standing at the edge of one of nature's widest open spaces. My heart rate rose, and I hadn't yet taken a step into the Canyon.

The mid-May air was crisp, and I was a bit nervous. Only our anxious voices cut the silence.

I was one of two dozen men set to embark on a daylong hike down the Canyon's rocky dirt switchbacks to the mouth of the Colorado River. The time estimate for the twelve-mile descent was between five and six hours. Once there, we would sit alongside the river with Nebraska head football coach Scott Frost to chat about new beginnings in the old neighborhood; about life, love, and leadership.

Frost is an elusive man whom I'd barely met. I had to chase him.

At the time he was a rising star in the collegiate coaching ranks, having just led the University of Central Florida to an undefeated 13-0 season and a statement Peach Bowl victory over Auburn. The year before Frost arrived at UCF, the Knights failed to win a single game. Two years into his tenure they won every game. That's one reason Frost was so sought after and so intriguing. When he formally accepted the challenge of returning his alma mater to the Tom Osborne–era glory days, his trajectory was vertical.

It felt right. Some of Osborne's greatest days as Nebraska's coach came during Frost's career as the Huskers' quarterback. Together, they led Nebraska to the 1997 National Championship, and Frost remains the lone native Nebraskan to quarterback the Huskers to a national title.

I tell you all of this to display his keen knowledge of the program's culture. He already knew the expectations. He already knew the platform—the entire state takes its identity from Big Red. For his entire youth, he did, too.

Frost had been on my radar since January 2018, when I met him on the sideline at the Mercedes-Benz Stadium in Atlanta, Georgia. He was at the College Football Playoff National Championship game, between Alabama and Georgia, to offer analysis on ESPN's *College GameDay* and detail why he chose to return to Nebraska.

He carried himself like a guy I'd like to drink a beer with. He has a quiet confidence that isn't cocky, direct without being condescending. He didn't strike me as one for posturing—an inclination that was confirmed when he invited my team and me to hike through the damn Grand Canyon with him in the middle of the night.

Most of the attendees on the Canyon expedition were college football coaches, with at least one lacrosse coach—University of Pennsylvania head coach Mike Murphy—sprinkled in. All but four of the participants would cross the Colorado and continue out the other side of the Canyon to the North Rim, completing a physically demanding twenty-four-mile trek that included more than five thousand feet of elevation change.

And they would do it all in one day.

The other foursome was our team at the time: cameraman/editor Sam Hoerdemann, audio technician Cory Harrilchak, producer Jonathan Whyley, and me. We've seen the world together, us four, along with Sam's father, Gregg, one of the great sports videographers of our time.

Together, we've piled four- and five-wide into single, cramped hotel rooms in foreign countries all across the globe, for entire weeks at a time, and worked around the clock with no sleep and no showers, fueled by cheekfuls of Red Man chewing tobacco and overpriced carafes of black coffee the consistency of motor oil, to supply unique and original content to the relentless consumer machine. Collectively, we've done stories in and across China, Italy, Mexico, Iceland, France, Austria, and Cuba, and in every corner of the United States of America.

In the process we have forged a unique working relationship, more of a brotherhood than simply coworkers, a bond I'd liken to a football team. We all are athletes, so we think and operate like athletes. Work tirelessly. Defy limits. Check your ego and your insecurities at the door. It ain't always pretty when victory is the mission.

For us, great stories, built upon great relationships, define victory. That's it. It sounds simple. It's not.

Between the lines, typical societal rules of engagement don't always apply. Some behavior deemed inappropriate or unacceptable in public is standard operating procedure between the lines. (When was the last time you smacked a coworker on the butt after a good board meeting? Or grabbed him by the tie and screamed at him to pull his head out of his ass after a bad one? You see both every single day throughout the sporting landscape.)

Between the lines, you lean on your brother. He picks you up when you fall, pushes you toward collective success when you individually fail. Unless family is involved, team is first, always. Prepare diligently. Preparation is something you can control. Demand it of yourself. Do your job to the absolute pinnacle of your ability, every time, every repetition, so that your brother has the same opportunity to perform at his optimum level, and thereby, collectively, you can achieve your greatest potential as a unit. (As we've stated previously in these pages, that, for all intents and purposes, is "the Process" according to Alabama head football coach Nick Saban.)

Between the lines, you fight sometimes. Jonathan and I have nearly gone to blows on multiple occasions. There was even a time once, deep within the Louvre in Paris, when the *Mona Lisa* watched us get so emotionally charged at each other that a tear rolled down my face. No lie. Rolled right down my cheek.

We were standing directly in front of the most famous painting on earth, completing one of those audio tours of the museum, and I was uncertain where to return my headset. We didn't have time to lollygag. When I mentioned to Whyley that I didn't know where to put the headset, he snapped something at me about interrupting the tour guide. Whether his tone was meant to be condescending or not, that's how I heard it, and it sent a dart directly into the bull's-eye of my insecurities. I wanted to knock him out.

My heart rate spiked and my blood pressure spiked, and since I could neither punch him nor yell at him—we were in the Louvre, for heaven's sake—I turned to walk away. I wanted to whip his ass right there in front of *Mona Lisa*, *Venus de Milo*, and Jim Harbaugh. I'm sure the feeling was mutual. Why? A mixture of pride, stupidity, intensity, and fatigue. That's the job.

We laugh about that moment now. In fact we were laughing about it that same night while editing over chew and coffee. Once the intensity of the mission cools, trials become tattoos, forever reminders that do not simply wash off with soap and water.

Our mentality as a group was exactly like that of a football team or a family: We could fight like hell with each other—but you'd be ill advised to ever try to fight us as a group. Oddly enough, that's also why we're successful, that intensity and unyielding push toward excellence and the intolerance of complacency.

I once asked Saban what he believed to be the greatest threat to sustained excellence. Without hesitation he responded: "Complacency." I love this Saban quote:

> When you're climbing a mountain, you look up. You never look back. Complacency is something that everyone who has any level of success must challenge themselves to overcome. But it's not just the willingness to do it. It's the why you're willing to do it. Because the why creates the passion for the what. And the passion creates the ability to sustain it.

I carry that quote with me every day as a reminder of my personal demand for excellence.

There is nothing complacent about hiking rim-to-rim in the Grand Canyon in one day. Our plan was to leave the coaches in the deepest part of the ravine, at a lodging area on the north side of the river called Phantom Ranch, which can be reached only by foot, by mule, or by rafting the Colorado.

We would then turn around and hike directly back across the river via the Silver Bridge, a thin steel suspension bridge, bolted into the canyon by long steel cables. The bridge was hardly wide enough to pass oncoming foot traffic, swayed back and forth with each step, and had a steel grate floor that allowed hikers to peer directly into the center of the river's current.

I hate heights. I didn't love that bridge.

Once back across, it was up those dusty switchbacks again to the South Rim entrance of the Canyon. Time did not allow us to continue on to the North Rim with the coaches. The drive from the North Rim to the South Rim required at least four hours. We couldn't spare the time. We had a red-eye to catch—and we needed those four hours to drive from the Canyon to Phoenix Sky Harbor Airport. I had no other option.

The next morning I had to be in our home city, Charlotte, North Carolina, to vote for the 2019 NASCAR Hall of Fame class. NASCAR demands that its voters attend in person. There are no exceptions and there shouldn't be. It's a privilege to sit in a room with my childhood heroes, titans like Richard Petty, Junior Johnson, and Ned Jarrett, debating greatness, to determine which stock-car-racing careers are worthy of eternal acclaim.

The day after that, I would fly to Indianapolis, Indiana, for five days to report on the 102nd running of the Indianapolis 500. I had to be on that 10:55 p.m. Phoenix-to-Charlotte red-eye.

To give an indication of how we shoehorned the Grand Canyon into our schedules: Two days before the hike marked the last of five days I spent in Baltimore, Maryland, at the Pimlico Race Course, documenting the second leg of the horse-racing Triple Crown. One day before the hike I was at the North River Yacht Club in Tuscaloosa, Alabama, to participate in the Crimson Tide Celebrity Golf Classic. Afterward, I rode in a minivan with New York Jets legend Marty Lyons and Atlanta Braves legend Fred McGriff to the airport in Birmingham, Alabama.

I flew from Birmingham, through Dallas, to Phoenix. After multiple cancellations and delays, I landed in Phoenix at 11:30 p.m. The hike was to begin in less than five hours. The boys scooped me up at PHX baggage claim and hammered the throttle toward Flagstaff.

Attempting to hike the entire way in a single day is discouraged because it is dangerous. But we took our philosophical approach from the keen perspective of the legendary poet T. S. Eliot: "Only those who risk going too far . . . find out how far they can go."

Our Grand Canyon journey would extend more than 26 miles and require more than 52,000 steps, as well as nearly 5,000 feet of uphill climbing. It would take more than thirteen hours, and test us physically, mentally, emotionally, personally, and collectively like nothing we'd ever experienced. It was the most difficult physical challenge I've experienced.

We later learned that people have died trying what we completed.

Our goal was to document the leadership exercise with Frost, led by former Marine Force Recon platoon commander Eric Kapitulik, whom most folks refer to as "Kap." Frost calls him "Kappy." So we called him "Kappy."

Kappy was one of Frost's close friends and founder of the Program, a leadership development and team-building service directed toward professional and collegiate sports teams. He used moments of shared adversity—like hiking the Grand Canyon—to teach leadership.

This was just the latest of Frost and Kappy's excursions together. They met when Frost was an assistant coach at Oregon. Frost took immediately to Kappy's philosophy and belief system. He liked being around men who challenged themselves beyond what they'd previously deemed to be capable. In recent years they had climbed seven New Hampshire mountain peaks, totaling more than twenty miles, in one day, and jumped into cages to swim with great white sharks in South Africa. And now the Canyon.

"Not many people can do this, and most of the people who can do it let fear run their lives," Kapitulik told me. "Many of those who can do this choose not to. They beat themselves. That's why, when I choose to hike across the Grand Canyon, and I wonder, 'Who will do this with me?' That's why I call Coach Frost. He's in. And he won't let fear beat him."

Kappy is a very intense dude, a bowling ball of a man with a bald head, a compact frame completely devoid of fat, and a motor that doesn't seem to ever stop, only idle periodically. He employs a zero-BS attitude. He is a genuine badass.

His "why" is harrowing. In 1999, during a routine training mission in preparation for deployment to the Persian Gulf, Kappy and his platoon mates were involved in a helicopter crash. Seven Marines died. In response, Kappy created a scholarship fund to benefit the children of his fallen men.

There were five young boys and one young girl who lost their fathers that day. On the strength of the Force Reconnaissance Scholarship Fund, the girl and two of the boys attended college. The others received career-starter loans to begin their professional lives.

After eight years of service, Kappy left active duty and earned his MBA from the University of Chicago graduate school. In 2008 he founded the Program. He's climbed Kilimanjaro and Everest. And a decade later there we stood, in the darkness, surrounded by elite leaders of men, listening to his commanding voice direct us.

"You can stand here and talk about it or you can do it," he yelled. "Let's go do it."

He's not the kind of guy you question. Off we went into the canyon.

One mile into the hike, we approached a warning sign alongside the cliffs on our right side. It was strategically positioned to ward against attempting exactly what we were about to attempt—down and back in one day. Park rangers wanted to be certain the message was delivered. Four different languages were represented on the sign—English, French, German, and Japanese.

The sign stood about six feet tall, and used an artistic drawing of a man on all fours puking his guts out to remind us that this hike was serious business. And that wasn't all the guy in the drawing did wrong. He was wearing cargo jorts, and for some reason no shirt. His back had been scorched by the sun's searing rays. He was also blond, leading Frost to quip that it looked just like him. He then turned to Kappy.

"We gotta be getting close to the end, right?"

For a guy with a reserved demeanor, Frost will unleash some zingers. Sometime around 7 a.m., I asked him if he'd ever been to the Canyon before. He hadn't, and noted to me how dumb he always thought it was to drive for hours or days to stand at the edge of a big hole, for what? Just to stare at it for three days? I found that comment to be absolutely hilarious.

For the first ninety minutes or so we didn't speak much. Then as the sun rose over the canyon and revealed the stunning topography and the considerable challenge ahead, I asked Frost why it was important for him to hike the entire Grand Canyon in the heat of the day.

What he said resonated with me.

"A leader should never ask his team to do anything he's not willing to do himself."

That's the quickest route to respect. Do as I say—*because I do.*

His insight centered on football principles. But it's applicable in many areas of life. It made me think about parenthood and brotherhood and marriage. Don't ask of your spouse, children, friends, or coworkers anything you won't do personally. Don't expect them to be accountable in ways you aren't. Practice what you preach.

As a dad I fail in those ways sometimes. I preach composure when my children face adversity, and then I fly off the handle—in front of them—when someone cuts me off in traffic. I expect patience *from* them, yet I'm often impatient *with* them. I expect them to speak to Lainie and me in a respectful tone, yet I sometimes find myself addressing them in an overbearing, unfair tone, even when I'm not upset.

It's interesting how we, as parents, seek to use our experiences to help our children avoid the mistakes we made. But somehow we forget that we made those mistakes. We were naive and absent-minded once. Sometimes I still am—like when I yell at them to get their faces out of the iPad . . . while I'm sending a text message.

I get annoyed that they aren't listening to me sometimes. Meanwhile, I can't imagine the unique and interesting things Lainie has shared with me over the years that I never heard because I had my face in my phone. (When she reads this she will roll her eyes.)

Rarely do coaches at Frost's level take a moment to pause and reflect, to climb out of their own canyons of recruiting, routines, game tape, and game plans to achieve a better understanding of who they are and what truly inspires them.

At the major college football level, winning is the only option, and the incessant push to ensure preparedness for the next challenge is all-consuming. Their lives speed by. And before they know it they've missed the blessing that is life.

To prepare for the hike, Frost had run Nebraska's Memorial Stadium steps while wearing a backpack with a twenty-five-pound weight inside. He had a bum ankle, scar tissue from an old basketball injury. But he trained doggedly. During our hike he told me he was in the worst shape of his life, and he explained many reasons why. That ankle, for one. The others all involved change.

Frost, forty-three years old at the time, was a new husband, to Ashley, and a new father, to their son, RJ, and all that came with it, sleeplessness, diapers, unconditional love, and unexpected perspective. He also had just made that aforementioned move from Orlando, Florida, to Lincoln, Nebraska. He was in the throes of recruiting new talent, assembling a coaching staff, and installing a new philosophy to achieve an old standard—winning.

"It's been a lot in the last year, but I couldn't ask for anything more," Frost said, seated beside me on a massive black rock, the Colorado River raging behind us. "Especially my first child being born, Ashley and I having a son.

"As many other good things have happened, nothing else even comes close to having your first child. It helps you as a coach. It helps you realize all the things you're working for are important, but they're not the number one priority. That frees you up to do your job even better."

That's where my head was as I shook Frost's hand, thanked him for his time and candor, and began to pack up for the return to the South Rim. Jonathan, Sam, Cory, and I left the coaches at Phantom Ranch at 9:30 a.m. By noon Sam and Cory were struggling. With good reason.

They had each lugged more than forty pounds of television equipment and gear down the mountain all morning, while bobbing and weaving and jumping and backpedaling to capture important footage for our piece. Jonathan and I carried standard backpacks.

Frost and Kappy continually mentioned how impressed—and concerned—they were regarding the weight the boys carried. Most participants had lightweight packs carrying three-liter water bladders and some food rations. And that's all they brought.

Our bunch didn't have much food. We found a couple of protein meal bars, left over from previous trips and airport delays, buried deep in the bottoms of our backpacks. But that was basically all we had, and we shared the bars among the four of us.

By no definition were we properly prepared. At one point, Sam and Cory saw a passerby eating some trail mix, the peanut, raisin, and M&M kind that never has a fair ratio of raisins to M&Ms. We asked if we could have it. All of it. Sam and Cory ate every morsel, thanked the passerby, and returned to her an empty plastic bag.

Hydration is the most important resource in the Grand Canyon. If you get dehydrated, you're done. Back before we left Phantom Ranch, we visited a little general store down by the river, which had fifteen or twenty sleeves of electrolyte hydration powder resting in a clear plastic jug on the counter. We bought the whole jug. At this same moment, seated on a picnic table, Whyley uncovered some sort of Vitamin B_{12} energy tablets in a white tube, little red disks created to dissolve in water. We chewed up the whole tube like Life Savers or Mentos. Without water.

I had two 20-ounce Dasani water bottles for the entire hike, purchased from a vending machine in the back corner of a Nowhere, Arizona, hotel lobby at 3:30 that morning. I think Jonathan had only one bottle. Fortunately, Sam and Cory have brains. They both had CamelBak packs that encased three-liter hydration bladders. All four of us shamelessly sucked water out of those packs for seven hours, and none of us paid any mind to the fact that we were sharing spit.

Typically we're germophobes who bathe in antibacterial cleanser and wipes. Not that day. That day was so physically taxing, we felt blessed just to have spit.

With two miles remaining in the expedition, the team separated into two groups—Sam and Cory, and Jonathan and me. We were all physically exhausted, sleep- and nutrition-deprived, and dehydrated worse than we realized. To make it home, we had to hike to the finish at our own desired paces.

For me, that was a quarter-mile shuffle to the next available knee-high rock, followed by a brief rest. Restarting after each rest period was awful. Standing up from a sharp rock piercing your ass cheek and coaxing the left foot in front of the right. It was a unique period psychologically, those final few miles. It was a time of self-preservation and self-examination.

I felt very small. I was reminded of God's wonder.

Finishing became the intersection where mental fortitude must override physical exhaustion and emotional immersion, and mind must convince body to carry on. The sun was rude. Eventually the sweat beads gave way to chills, which was counterintuitive in the heat of the day. It was also very scary, an indicator that dehydration was very real.

By this time we were completely disinterested in the stunning, humbling beauty surrounding us. It was vital to focus directly on placing one foot in front of the other, because fatigue promoted wandering focus. And the terrain was such that a wandering focus could result in broken ankles from false steps on loose rocks, stumbles over tall logs, or tumbles from the edge of steep, jagged cliffs.

If you didn't respect it, it would choose against respecting you.

We dodged teams of a dozen donkeys or more, connected at the saddles by ropes, galloping down the mountain, carrying gleeful tourists wearing wide-brimmed sun hats, toothy smiles, and remarkably clean shorts and T-shirts. I found it odd how happy and spry and clean they were versus how miserable we felt. We had forty pounds of gear on our backs and dust-stained clothes. We weren't laughing.

This day was Vivian's sixth birthday, May 22. I hate missing my kids' birthdays. It makes me feel like an absent father. One mile from the top, I took some selfie video footage atop a ridge to send to her. I wished her a happy birthday and reminded her how precious she was to me and that I couldn't wait to hug and kiss her.

A bandanna, beige and yellow and orange, emblazoned with the Canyon horizon, purchased hours before back at Phantom Ranch, surrounded my forehead and covered the tips of my ears. A hat I'd bought months before at the Masters was perched atop my head. My face was slathered with zinc oxide sunscreen. Whatever it took to keep the sun off me. My voice cracked in the video. I choked back tears.

Lainie never showed Vivian that birthday video. I was gaunt and pale with distant eyes, and she was afraid Vivian would be scared seeing her daddy that way.

Whyley and I walked together for much of that final push. He shouldered the heaviest pack at first. We estimated it weighed fifty pounds. It held audio gear, microphones, our main "shotgun" camera, and several large, heavy camera batteries, as well as an ever-shrinking hydration bladder.

Eventually he was exhausted enough to consider a trade. He's hardheaded as the devil and in good physical condition, so his fatigue was telling. I handed him the thirty-five-pound bag and took the fifty-pounder.

He and I are not big men. We both weigh about 160 pounds. Carrying a third of your body weight up a mountain is rowdy. I shuffled my feet all the way home, quadriceps, hamstrings, and hip flexors burning, knees and feet aching. I was barely able to walk. That is not hyperbole.

At 4:30 p.m. Mountain Time, I walked out of the South Rim exit of the Grand Canyon. I couldn't find Whyley and couldn't walk anymore, so I simply collapsed on what appeared to be a new, clean white concrete sidewalk, and I leaned hard on that fifty-pound pack on my back.

There were folks in shorts and T-shirts milling about, cameras dangling from their necks, designer sunglasses glinting in the afternoon sun, staring a hole through me like I was deranged. I suddenly had a new respect for what lions caged in the zoo must feel like.

And at that moment, as they slurped their sodas and crammed ice-cream cones into their mouths, I was reminded that photographs and video do not tell the Grand Canyon story. Unless you see it, you haven't seen it. And unless you've hiked it, you haven't truly experienced it.

I smiled at something Kappy had told me hours and miles before, as we approached the mouth of the mighty Colorado, which perfectly encapsulated my feeling of accomplishment in that moment:

"Most people stand up there and stare down into the canyon. Very few stand down here and look up it," he said. "You can extrapolate this to most of life: The Grand Canyon is beautiful when you're standing on top, looking down. It just means more when you're on the bottom looking up."

"Cut & Paste"

We all make mistakes we want back. Wouldn't it be nice sometimes if we could rectify human screwups as easily as we rectify electronic ones?

Cut & Paste

On my computer I made a mistake...
So I decided to cut and paste...
I wish some mistakes I've made in my life...
Were that easy to replace...
Or just erase.

Chapter Twenty-Three

May We Ever Aspire

Though I typically only saw him during the holidays in my formative years, one of the important influences on my life and moral compass was my maternal grandfather, the Reverend James Massey. My mom's dad. He was a Baptist minister, beloved for his patience and perspective, lauded and awarded by the Southern Baptist Convention for his leadership. Stacy and I called him "Hershey Bar Jim" because every time we visited him as kids there was a pair of full-size Hershey bars waiting for us in the refrigerator, the kind you unsheathe from fine-pressed foil and can snap apart into smaller miniature Hershey bars. Well into my adult years, if Papa Jim knew I was coming to Richmond to visit, he bought a Hershey bar for me.

I grew up in the church. Mom was our choir director. So until I was old enough to drive, the weekly routine was church on Sunday morning, youth group on Sunday night, choir practice on Wednesday night, potluck supper on Saturday. Folks came by the house often to practice hymns and songs with Mom. One of my favorites was "Children Go Where I Send Thee," a fast-paced hymn that Mom sang while she played an acoustic guitar. It was awesome to see her perform. She carried an air of confidence up on the stage that we didn't always see otherwise. I marveled at how perfectly she remembered the lyrics and placed them perfectly within the song's rapid cadence—"one for the little bitty baby...Born! Born! Born in Bethlehem..."

Fortunately, my buddies' parents were just as integrated into the church as Mom was, so while our folks prepared for Sunday's service, we played football or basketball in the church basement. We did a number on that church basement, "dunking" mini basketballs into the low-slung ceiling or tackling each other into the walls or the folding picnic-style chairs surrounding the walls.

As I wrote earlier in this book, my mother, Joy, was an unmistakable Christian example for Stacy and me. She was kind to everyone, and had overwhelming empathy. She learned that approach from her parents.

Papa Jim, as his grandkids called him, was the godliest man I've ever known. He was completely nonjudgmental and welcomed all comers, regardless of race, creed, strife, or obstacle, and without predisposed bias when a particular viewpoint differed from his. That's a very rare trait. He looked at God's Word in a functional sense and applied it to every decision he made and conviction he carried. Until I was much older we had nothing in common. Papa Jim was not interested in sports or popular music—which were the only things I was interested in for most of my young life. But he prayed for me every day, and eventually for Lainie and our kids, too. He told me so each time we talked. I'm absolutely certain that is one reason I'm so blessed.

Papa Jim served in World War II, as a member of General George S. Patton's Third Army, the 80th Infantry Division, and he lived by Patton's famous leadership philosophy:

"Do everything you ask of those you command."

In other words, walk the walk.

James Cambron Massey always walked the walk.

For example, to my knowledge Papa Jim never had a sip of alcohol. But he never judged or chastised any of us for enjoying a cold beer. (And man, we like cold beer.) He didn't appreciate us drinking, not one bit. But he didn't lecture us, either. He didn't have to. We knew how he felt.

At the very same time, he couldn't have been prouder to be the great-grandson of Dan Call, a Tennessee Lutheran minister in the mid-1800s, who also owned a general store and distilled a little brown liquor out back. A young boy worked for Reverend Call in that store, and Call taught him the whiskey trade. Eventually, Call hit a crossroads that required him to choose the whiskey or the Word. He chose to stay with his church congregation, and he sold the whiskey business to the boy.

That boy's name—get this—was Jack Daniel.

That's right: My great-great-grandfather, Reverend Daniel Call, had a hand in inventing Jack Daniel's Whiskey. The Old No. 7. My buddies love to clown me mercilessly about that story. They refuse to believe it. I've actually fought a couple of those idiots over it. Now, admittedly, I haven't jumped on any ancestry websites or scoured the library in Lynchburg, Tennessee, to confirm the lineage. But my granddaddy never lied to me about anything. I can't imagine he'd start with liquor. There's a book called *Jack Daniel's Legacy* that spells it all out. It mentions our ancestors. Papa Jim took a highlighter to the passages of his tattered copy that mentioned our family. It was passed on to me when he died.

Back to the war.

Two days before Christmas in 2009, I sat quietly on the same couch that had played host to the countless wistful, lazy afternoons of my youth. It was red, the cotton-duck sort of material that is scratchy until worn. As napping couches go, it was unrivaled. It gradually pulled you in and you wondered how you'd ever get back out. It was like a cotton quicksand bed.

Throughout my childhood and into adolescence I lived in perpetual motion; hyper isn't nearly a strong enough description. I truly could not sit still. I drove Momma crazy in church, constantly shifting my position in the pew or begging her for a mouthful of Life Savers. One particularly annoying activity was grabbing a handful of adhesive nametags reserved for church visitors, writing my name (illegibly) on every last one of them, and sticking them all over my forehead, my shirt, the pew cushion, or my buddies' backs.

I once saw a home video of nine-year-old me at Christmastime. I looked like a drunk hornet in a hamster cage, buzzing around aimlessly and running headfirst into everything in its path—just confused and amused enough to keep doing it.

But as I eased into my teens I began to appreciate the simple beauty of the midafternoon slumber. Especially at my grandparents' home in Richmond, Virginia. I sat and pondered this on that wintry day in 2009. But this time there would be no nap or relaxation. I was nervous.

The evening sky was dumping record amounts of snow on Richmond and most of the rest of the Northeast. Lainie and I, and our two young children at the time, stopped over at my grandparents' home for a visit en route to New Jersey to celebrate the Christmas holiday.

This was customary. Before my grandparents died, we stopped every time we trudged north through the I-95 carnival. It provided a nice stopping point, a visit with family I rarely saw, and the amazing dynamic of witnessing great-grandparents and great-grandchildren interact. Watching my ninety-something-year-old grandfather bounce my nine-month-old daughter on his knee was an astounding experience. Both giggled at nothing more than each other's company.

Amid the laughter and fellowship I was anxious. I had decided I would broach the subject of World War II with my grandfather. I was uncertain how he would react. As a preacher he was a teacher, always open to using his own life experiences to illustrate God's plan in a broader scope. But whether he would openly discuss hell on earth was impossible to predict.

I figured not.

But I was born to try, no matter how impossible something may seem.

In recent years I had twice read Tom Brokaw's *The Greatest Generation*. The individual tales of ordinary people doing extraordinary things inspired me deeply. There is rich beauty in the everyday for those willing to seek it. Thing is, few folks are willing to ask. Brokaw did. And he found it. In doing so, he uncovered a common theme among World War II veterans, the general distaste for trumpeting their service. It was rarely discussed.

Going to war was what Uncle Sam had asked them to do, and by God, they did it. That's all anyone really needed to know about it. End of story. But that's immeasurably far from the end of the story for the millions of us who benefited from that selflessness. Each of these men and women personally contributed to the post-Depression rebirth of the greatest nation on earth. Our nation. The United States of America. And each of them has a story worthy of telling and hearing.

There was no doubt in my mind that my grandfather had an important story. He is such a gracious man, and he has long been the standard toward which I point my moral compass. That by no means insinuates I come close to his standard. I do not. I always felt like my grandfather lived at the altar, and I was somewhere between the church pew and the barstool.

I knew he had served his country, but I'd never taken an interest in asking him about it. Like many kids of the '80s, I was too self-absorbed to respect the sacrifice required of our ancestors to create this land of opportunity. In fact, I was oblivious. When everything you could ever desire is right at your fingertips, you don't concern yourself with what it took to create that life.

Then I lost both parents. When that happens, a man gets introspective real quick. I was thirty-two years old, and I had begun to develop a new concept of discovering who I really was, and why, while refusing to settle for "good enough."

I was driving down Highway 460 in Virginia one evening in May 2008—I had just lost my daddy a month prior—and a song came upon the radio. It was "In Color" by Jamey Johnson, a country music throwback to the Waylon Jennings–Johnny Cash era. I drove and I listened. It was emotional for me. In the song, Johnson details his grandparents' lives, how that generation grew up poor and fought for an intangible truth far bigger than they could imagine, then worked like hell to preserve it and were proud of it their entire lives.

The song spoke to me. I knew then I owed it to my grandfather to ask about his service. He was an American hero. I knew I owed it to my mom, to myself, and to my children. Time was short.

I sat there on the edge of that red couch, adjacent to the weathered leather recliner with the broken footrest from which he had presided over the establishment since I was a toddler, and I asked him meekly to tell me about World War II.

I listened, captivated and inquisitive, as he told old war stories. *Dora the Explorer* blared in the background as my four-year-old played on the floor. My grandmother, Frankie Pearl Henderson Massey—we called her Mimi—sat beside him, to his right, in a wooden chair, just as she had every night for decades.

Papa Jim spoke for six hours. He chuckled often, wept more.

I captured his words on a small black tape recorder. That tape recorder was taken from me while I checked in once for jury duty. Thinking about that now makes me angry and nauseous. I could puke. Fortunately I had already transcribed much of our conversation. I just wish I could still hear it.

He noted that after the Japanese bombed Pearl Harbor on December 7, 1941, the sense of patriotism in America was very strong. His chin rested on his chest. He was staring at the floor.

"Like everyone else I was distressed over it, because America had felt it had been violated," he told me that night in 2009. "I don't think we ever expect to be invaded on our shores in the way we were at Pearl Harbor. And the horror of the suddenness and the awful carnage was very difficult for us to take in, because it did happen here. Not some far-off land. It was right here, in our country."

As he spoke, Mimi mostly stared blankly at the floor, too. I wondered whether the stories were painful for her to recall or if, possibly, this was her first time hearing them, too. Surely not.

But she never flinched. Just listened. At times she closed her eyes and covered her mouth with her hand as if to deeper hone her focus on Papa Jim's words. She had long been his sounding board. I could tell his words caused her pain.

Papa Jim detailed one particularly miserable night spent bivouacking in a French forest. It was sopping wet everywhere. It had rained for days, and the trucks and other vehicles had ground up the earth about them. It was wretched.

The one saving grace that evening came in the form of a pup tent, not even as big as a double bed and as leaky as an old faucet. He explained that even the slightest shift in body weight resulted in a freezing shower of rain. The soldiers weren't always permitted to erect a tent, but on this night they granted that luxury. So Papa Jim and his fellow chaplain put one up, staked down on both sides and open in the front, and then shared it.

It was barely big enough for both of them.

In the next field over, there was a battery of 150 mm Howitzers. They fired constantly, shaking the ground with every launch. The horrible weather and incessant Howitzer strikes, while being so far from home and away from Frankie, and the fact that German 88 airplanes were constantly raining counterfire upon those Howitzers, made James question himself.

"I was lying there, wide awake and as miserable as I could ever recall being, and I said to myself, 'What on earth am I doing here? *What on earth am I doing here?*' Over and over. And does anybody know? And does anybody even care?'"

Remembering it was difficult. He paused often to collect himself. I felt like I was prying.

"There was an old gospel song called 'Does Jesus Care?'" he continued. "I remembered the words to that first stanza, and I remembered the chorus. And I sang them to myself. The words said, 'Oh yes He cares. I know He cares. His heart is touched by your grief.'"

Despite the misery all around him, James turned over and fell sound asleep. He was exhausted, mentally, emotionally, and physically.

In the days thereafter, he happened upon what he said might be the most telling of his memories from the war. His unit was bivouacked in a building of some sort, and he walked outside for some fresh air. There was a German bunker that held a machine gun nest, and at least five German soldiers were still lying inside, dead.

One was sprawled on his back, his arm flung out.

He was wearing a wedding ring.

Papa Jim said he found himself overcome with compassion for the enemy.

"I said to myself, 'There but for the grace of God, I am.'"

There is a scene in the movie *Patton* that James knew all too well. Because he lived it.

His unit was in southern Germany, and got word that the Battle of the Bulge had begun. Patton's army was ordered to join the battle, and was to ride through the night and directly through the constant threat of German bombing raids. At that same time, Patton ordered the chief of chaplains to write a prayer that God would guard and protect the convoy.

It was a stark admission of vulnerability by a man who rarely ever showed any.

It had been snowing and the ground was covered, which made the skies bright enough that the convoy could drive fairly safely without lights. Then, lo and behold, the fog rolled in, making it impossible for German planes to fly. At that moment, Patton ordered the convoy to turn on the lights and stand on the gas pedal.

It was quite a blessing, indeed. Recalling the pride in Papa Jim's delivery of that story gives me chills.

The convoy rolled into Luxembourg the following morning, and Papa Jim's unit was bivouacked in a summer palace of the duchess of Luxembourg. They may as well have fallen face-first into the Four Seasons. He described the building as magnificent, with marble floors, wide staircases, and marble balustrade. There was very little furniture, as everything had already been moved out. James and the boys slept on the floor.

The marble was as hard as concrete, but it was a Sealy Posturepedic compared to that cold, wet French forest. They had a roof, after all.

What little furniture was left was covered. It was gorgeous, gilded, and elegant, stationed in a magnificent ballroom. This particular home was special to Papa Jim. He spent the Christmas of 1944 there.

The French orchard and the "Prayer Ride" were among count-less moments during World War II that would indelibly impact my grandfather's life and faith. In fact, every day pretty much pro-vided at least one such example.

Typically as the convoy made its way through the countryside there was concern of mines. The Allied Forces sought to keep the roads swept, but there was no way to know for sure. Sometimes they would drive through battle areas that had recently been moved on, and there were dead horses, dead cows—dead people—lying mangled alongside the road.

Some of them had been bulldozed aside. There was no time for roadblocks.

Roadblocks slowed the convoy.

The general disregard for human fragility troubled Papa Jim. Many of his contemporaries numbed to death almost immedi-ately. He never did.

In Germany, during the Battle at Bastogne, James's unit visited a grave registration point. These units made sure soldiers killed in battle abroad were identified and received a proper burial. The soldiers' personal items were noted and returned to their families back home. In Luxembourg, bodies of soldiers, American boys, who were killed in the fighting were laid out to be placed in body bags. They were stripped of clothing, completely nude. Some were mangled. James remembered a white, blond-haired fellow. And a black fellow. And an Asian fellow.

"The equality in that mortality—all being Americans—was very moving," he said. "I will never forget that. It was the most remark-able moment of equality I'd ever seen. In that pile they were all the same."

James's unit did not stop. They moved along.

They did not participate in funerals. It was not their job.

The Graves Registration team did a good job removing American soldiers from battle sites. But the Germans remained, some in burned-out tanks, bodies hanging out the turret. There were bodies in the ditches, too, heads half shot off, alive with maggots.

"It gets hard not to hate when you see that sort of thing," he told me.

He also never forgot the day his unit visited a concentration camp at Ohrdruf, Germany. They arrived the day after the camp had been liberated. While there, James ventured down a road in his Jeep, and came to a T intersection. He made a left-hand turn at the intersection and, of all people on the planet, Frankie's brother Paul came walking up that road.

Sixteen million American soldiers served in World War II—two million fought in Europe alone—and he ran into his brother-in-law at an intersection in Germany.

Ironically, he said, he nearly took a right.

Papa Jim told these stories well into the night, some humorous, most harrowing. He was honest and vulnerable.

James Cambron Massey spent nineteen months in Europe as a member of Patton's Third Army. The lessons he learned there, both psychological and spiritual, forced him to lean heavily on God for promise and guidance, and also for some semblance of understanding as to why war was the right answer to solving conflict.

He didn't believe in war. But he believed in America.

God invariably answered, leading James to join the ministry immediately upon returning to civilian life. He was an extraordinary man, and he married an extraordinary woman.

My grandparents were married for seventy-three years. Their love was indomitable. They verbalized it.

Before, during, and immediately after the war until they were reunited, Papa Jim wrote Mimi nearly every day. Sometimes more than once a day. He was an altruistic man. Some letters reached her. Some didn't. During his stay overseas, Papa Jim explained to me that censorship was paramount. No shipped letters meant no leaked secrets. The letters from overseas, particularly, were of stark contrast, beautiful swooping cursive strokes laid upon drab Army-issue stationery. He wrote on both sides. Army-issue stationery was scarce.

I have many of those letters. My hope was to write a book based on their messages. Maybe someday. Before my grandparents handed the letters over to me, they reread them all to make sure they weren't too personal or revelatory. I guess Papa Jim must have written some risqué love notes. That made me laugh. And it made my grandparents belly laugh. It was a beautiful sound.

The following is an excerpt from one of those letters. My grandfather wrote it after being drafted into the United States Army. It offers an idea of how deeply in love he was with my grandmother, and where his mind was as he considered heading to war.

May 29, 1942; Nashville, Tennessee

Dearest Frankie,

The aching is caused, I think, by a nervous strain and worry. She remembers I am going away, and thinks of it, and cries. Sweetheart, the moon is beautifully romantic here tonight, nice and round, peeping through the trees very teasingly. I wish we were together beneath it. Goodnight, my dear, and may we both dream of years of happiness, years of peace and security, years of delightful work, years when all vain desires, false hopes, and longing fade into nothingness, years of happy unity, of two aspiring souls—may God grant these years and may we ever aspire.

James

"May we ever aspire." What a line. It is a reminder to strive, to seek, to love, to wonder, and to try. And to never settle.

Chapter Twenty-Four

Never Settle

In the winter of 2014, Laura Turk, the alumni relations director at my alma mater, Radford University, asked me to deliver the graduation commencement address to the Highlander Class of 2015.

I was thrilled and honored, for myself and for my wife, herself a Radford alumna, and immediately accepted the invitation. It was humbling to even be considered. I appreciated Laura's belief that I could deliver a quality, memorable speech. Not everyone involved in the decision was so sure. Some folks wanted a politician.

Unless it's a former president or vice president, nobody remembers a politician.

I don't have a fancy title or any measure of fame. So some of the RU academics had never heard of me. But the students knew. Because I was them. Years before, I had sat in those exact seats on that exact lawn in the sprawling courtyard outside the Moffett Hall dormitory, and I listened to a guy whose name I can't recall deliver a message I don't remember. He was a politician.

For the most part the commencement circuit is formulaic. But every now and then someone comes along and within twenty minutes speaks a legacy into the annals of leadership principles.

Like retired Admiral William H. McRaven, ninth commander of the US Naval Special Operations Command. His address at the University of Texas on May 17, 2014, is a copyright. It lives forever and it is his forever, because it is universally applicable and indisputable.

Make your bed.

"If you want to change the world, start off by making your bed," Admiral McRaven told those Longhorns. "If you can't do the little things right, you'll never do the big things right."

Man! That statement was so simple. But dynamic and true.

Admiral McRaven approached his twenty minutes with those students as a mission, and he won. It was a lasting victory over complacency.

Delivering a quality message to a sea of young people on a hot spring morning—who, let's face it, really just want to go drink beers with their friends and celebrate one of life's indelible moments—was a big responsibility. I took that challenge very seriously. I was nearly forty years old at the time. But I distinctly remembered how it had felt to sit right where those graduates sat.

I was bored, man. It shouldn't have been that way.

The speech at my graduation didn't resonate with me. Admittedly, I didn't pay attention the way I should have. I was intent on wrapping up the formalities quickly, stripping the cap and gown, and hanging out with Lainie and my buddies. I was also distracted. My mom was very sick. Her cancer had advanced to the point that she required hospice care back in Pearisburg. She couldn't attend the ceremony.

Daddy was very proud of me on the day I graduated from college. He said it but he struggled to show it, because he was overwhelmed with grief from watching his wife suffer in a rollaway bed in the center of his living room. He was defeated, depressed, sad, and angry. I, too, was full of anger and frustration and the intangible need to blame something. But I held it all inside. I still do, more than twenty years later. It's not healthy. Lainie tells me that. But it's my way to cope.

Sometimes while driving down the highway, the Juice Newton song "Angel of the Morning" comes on the radio. I turn it up too loud and sometimes cry. Mom used to sing that song to Stacy and me. I love that song. It's a piece of Mom for me.

That brings me back to the speech. I thought about all those variables as I stepped to the podium to address thousands of young people who were managing their own real-life problems. I had goals: Make the audience laugh, cry, think, learn, appreciate, remember, and, above all, pay attention.

I cared deeply about that fifteen-minute speech. Because if I did it right, those fifteen minutes could impact a life.

Lainie and I made an amazing day of it. Many of our best friends from college returned to Radford to support me and to enjoy a reunion of sorts. Corey Reed and Steve Bailey, both groomsmen for me on the day I married Lainie, flew in from Houston and Milwaukee, respectively. Another of my groomsmen, Kevin Robinson, one of the greatest basketball players in Radford history, drove over from Richmond, along with our friends Emily and Russ Turner.

Lindsay and Wendell Jones drove five hours round-trip from Kingsport, Tennessee, just to see me and hear me speak for a few minutes. They had another engagement to attend that same evening, but they came anyway. They're those kinds of friends. Make time for everybody. Jody and Tammie Steger showed up, and later opened their nearby lake house to us for a wee-hours beer-and-bonfire throwdown. I am so blessed to have friends like these.

Once the ceremony ended, the party began. We walked as a group from one side of the campus to the other, crashed parties, bummed beers, and visited the homes Lainie and I lived in while we were in school. Naturally, there were rowdy parties at both dwellings. We chugged beers with the graduates. I was surprised to learn that the men's soccer team lived at my old haunt, 527 Fairfax Street. They were equally surprised when we strolled down Fairfax on foot, rolled right up onto the front porch, grabbed a beer, and hung out awhile. They took me on a tour of the house and back in time.

Lainie and I cherish the memory of that day. We always will.

In the years since, I've received many inspiring letters and enjoyed many kind comments about that speech. One of the more notable and meaningful came out of nowhere from my former colleague Andy Petree, who was once Dale Earnhardt's NASCAR Championship crew chief, and whom I worked alongside at ESPN for eight years.

I was leaving the Daytona 500 prerace drivers meeting in the racetrack's infield when Andy walked up. At the time he held an executive role at Richard Childress Racing, one of the NASCAR teams. He is a handsome man with a great smile and an infectious laugh. As we walked through a parking lot toward the Cup Series garage, he turned to me and asked me to stop for a minute.

He said he watches my commencement speech several times each year, because it deeply inspires him and stokes the coals of his inner fire. That floored me. Tears welled in my eyes. I was so proud to learn that information. Andy didn't have to say it, but the message moved him enough that he wanted me to know.

This is the 2015 Radford University commencement speech, exactly as written, which was delivered on May 9, 2015, before some ten thousand attendees.

I wish Momma had been there to hear it.

NEVER SETTLE

Hello, everyone... As was stated, my name is Marty Smith.

Radford University Class of 1998. Yes, I am a fossil...

Though I speak publicly for a living, I cannot articulate to you guys how humbling it is for me to be here with you today. It is a tremendous honor.

I have the sweetest memories of this place. They live in a Polaroid sort of fashion…generally foggy but with intense bursts of great clarity and vibrancy. I found love here. Found direction. Found opportunity.

Lifelong friends…

Drank my first beer and met my wife at the same frat party, same night. Delta Chi. Beast Ice. Whew…That stuff'll leave you wondering what direction the train came from—and where it took the rest of you…

I'm really proud to be an alumnus of this university. You should be too. Fifteen years ago—we'll call it fifteen—I WAS you. I sat right here on this very lawn…and listened to someone I can't recall try to tell me about the world and how to succeed in it.

All I wanted to do was go drink beers with my buddies. So I know where your head is today and I respect it. This is a day to celebrate. When you're twenty-two years old… sitting and listening to some old man go on and on is exasperating. I was that way once, too. I'm not anymore. I've come to learn that those who came before me are far wiser and far more interesting.

They've lived it. Been there, done that.

I've lived what you've lived. Not that I'm especially interesting.

Liberty got Jeb Bush today.

VA Tech got a Google executive.

Y'all got me.

Point: Radford!

I'm just a guy who reports about sports for a living. That is my job. Not my identity. I'm a father. I'm a husband.

I'm a friend. I'm a brother. Today's message is not about professional excellence.

To me, professional excellence lives at the intersection between passion and preparedness.

If you work harder than the next guy and you're kind to people along the way...professional excellence is attainable for anybody.

And if anyone tells you different, it's because they don't live at that intersection. Their motor wouldn't take them there.

Once you reach that intersection it's all about passion, desire, and opportunity. All three are vital.

Let's talk opportunity for a minute

Here in a few minutes you'll have a Radford diploma. Be proud of that. It's no small feat. Someone told me recently that they had concern about the perception that a Radford degree is somehow inferior to those from other schools. This person was concerned that folks don't feel a Radford degree is quite so impressive. Here's a news flash: Anybody who thinks that is an idiot.

You think a Radford degree doesn't measure up? Turn on *SportsCenter.* I'll be waiting. You think a Radford degree doesn't measure up? Call Marquette's golf office and talk to Coach Steve Bailey, RU class of '98. He was in my wedding. One of my best friends. He's from here. He just led Marquette to the Big East Championship. He's done just fine with a Radford diploma. Don't think a Radford degree measures up? Call Corey Reed, RU class of '98. Best man in my wedding. He's a chemical engineer down in Houston now for ExxonMobil. He's smarter than you are. And he's smarter than most of those people with fancier degrees. His Radford degree is serving him just fine.

Any degree is an opportunity. That piece of paper cracks the door. It doesn't matter if it says Radford. Harvard. Duke. Virginia Tech. Don't care. That degree cracks the door to the opportunity.

From there it's up to you to kick that damn door down.

Let no one compromise your belief that you can do that. No door stands in your way. I don't care where you're from, what your social or economic backgrounds are. In a few minutes you will have a college diploma.

A college diploma is a key that starts a car. All keys differ. Some start Ferraris and some start Granny's Cutlass 88. Some are faster than others, but they all move you toward the destination you choose and it's up to you to find its limits.

I pushed every limit.

I grew up in a tiny little town in Nowhere, Virginia, got a degree from a state school, got a job that paid thirteen grand, waited for the next crack in the door, kicked the damn thing down.

The world's tough these days.

Life is one big deadline.

Succeed under immense pressure.

Don't stumble.

Lead, don't follow.

Stand out but don't.

I don't envy you guys. Straight up. If I graduated today, there would be no me. That $13,000 job doesn't exist today. At least I got a job. Newspapers don't have the budgets they once did. Some have died. Some of you will face that same thing. Talent. Desire. Where's the opportunity?

So how do you guys, the Class of 2015, get that job and keep that job and excel to the next job? Be fearless. I was. And I was just stupid enough to believe every dream I had was attainable. God almighty that's naive. But is it? Nobody ever told me different.

A couple years ago I was at a seminar up at ESPN. There was a guy up at the front of the room charged with telling us to stay in our lanes. What? Hell no! To me, stay in your lane means do your job, don't let anybody by you, don't take chances... Take a conservative approach.

Don't veer too far left or too far right. Be linear not abstract.

When that guy said that comment, I checked out. Right there. Done.

Stay in your lane? Obviously that works for some folks. Some folks stay in their lanes and enjoy a wonderful life. But don't you dare let anybody tell you to stay in your lane if you have aspirations otherwise.

How many folks who shaped history stayed in their lane? Do you think Steve Jobs stayed in his lane? Some of you guys are bored already, five minutes in, texting your girlfriend or your buddies on a fancy new iPhone 6. Imagine if Steve Jobs stayed in his lane. You would just be sitting there bored all alone with rested thumbs.

Do you think George Patton stayed in his lane? Would we be free to live in the greatest land in the world without his tremendous, and quite unconventional, leadership in World War II? We're lucky we don't know the answer to that. He said, "We herd sheep, we drive cattle, we lead people. Lead me, follow me, or get out of my way."

Did Johnny Cash or the Ramones or Bruce Springsteen or Lady Gaga stay in their lane? No. Imagine what they—and we—would have lost had they so chosen to stay in their lane.

These days, the way I see it, if you stay in your lane, you're getting passed. Yarded. Because today's world is not a two-way street. People aren't waiting around for you or abiding by a double-yellow line. Today's world is a ten-lane highway running one hundred miles per hour with a middle finger in the air.

Everybody here is probably active on myriad forms of social media. These days companies have monetized it. Everything lives real-time at 140 characters a second.

That's why you should write thank-you notes

It matters. I write them to everybody. And they remember. You want to stand out in the one-hundred-mile-per-hour rat race? Slow down a minute. Pull out a pen. Time spent with that pen separates you from the pack. In a world of texts and tweets and immediacy, minutes spent with that pen buy you years in a man's memory.

Learn to listen

If you learn to listen, it will benefit you. That one took me some time, time I'd like to save you. Listen. Your parents, coworkers, friends, siblings, they have interesting things to say.

Be selfless and attentive in that way. Shut up and listen. You'll be better for it. Some of the greatest leaders of our history are great listeners. And in today's world of constant posturing and fill-the-air banter, great listeners stand out.

Good listeners demand attention and command respect. If you're always jabber-jawing, folks tune it out. If you're selective, they're invariably attentive.

That's one reason I'm where I am in sports journalism. I speak when my interview subject finishes his or her thought. I wasn't always so patient. Know who taught me that? Dale Earnhardt Jr. I'd done an interview with Jeff Gordon, and I was quite proud of it, thought it was really strong.

But I'd cut Jeff off a few times, didn't listen well, didn't let the conversation breathe and ponder the cadence. Later that day I was interviewing Earnhardt and he told me I needed to shut up and stop interrupting, that Gordon had started some thoughts Junior really wanted to hear. And I didn't allow for it because I wouldn't shut up.

Man, I felt awful. I was pissed and I was embarrassed.

But I stashed that away.

Constructive criticism. Don't posture. Improve. Take that and look in the mirror with it. The mirror doesn't lie. People are gonna criticize you. That's America. If you reach a position of authority, people are gonna kiss your ass. That's America.

You can use both as fuel but neither as currency

That mirror will tell you the truth. When it's you and your eyes, your eyes hold the cards.

Radford's greatest impact on me was the people. The people that invested in me here had far greater impact than the classes did. Folks like Mike Ashley, Rick Rogers, Dave Hunziker, and Lynn Phillips grew me up. I love them. Every one. They built my self-esteem in a time when I really needed it. They trusted me to get real-world work done. Their necks were on the line for trusting me so much. I'm forever grateful for that experience. I don't know why they believed. But they believed. I felt that belief, and I've tried to pay it forward. I urge you to help others. It is the greatest professional reward in this life.

So if you had a professor, a teacher, an adviser, coach, friends…that made your college experience especially memorable…that believed in you…that championed your dream and your passion, you find them today…you thank them today…I'm fortunate I get to do that now, nearly twenty years later…

When I think about Radford I think about acceptance, searching for who I was and who I wanted to be. Just so you know, I'm still looking. It was my time to be young and wild and stupid, and dress dumb and act dumber.

You won't realize the impact of your growth as a person here until later on. That's life. You go and move and do and be until moments become years and years decades and then you're standing at the counter one day making school lunches for your brood at 5:45 in the morning going, Man, Momma died seventeen years ago.

Then you'll think about a moment that makes you smile and a moment that makes you weep and a moment that makes you wonder why you did it, how you did it, and why it worked.

Be confident but not egotistical

Let's talk ego a minute. Ego will bury you. I've seen it compromise marriages. I've seen it destroy friendships. I've seen it end careers. If there's any level of lessons-learned wisdom I want you to take away from today, it's very simple: Work hard. Be kind.

For as far back as I can remember, my momma beat the Golden Rule into me. **Treat others the way you want to be treated.** Don't compromise that. Work has cliques. You think high school had cliques? Work is high school high.

If you outwork the next guy and you're graceful in doing it, the rest will manage itself. Trust me. I've lived it.

I've learned through time that humility and self-confidence walk hand in hand. Cockiness is often posturing from something that's missing.

Your skill set might be better than the next guy's. But you're not better than the next guy. Be proud but not prideful. That degree matters. Some of you have parents that worked to the bone so you could walk this stage today. They sacrificed, many times and in many more ways than you could possibly fathom, for you to walk this stage. So if your momma and your daddy are here with you today, or granny or aunt or uncle, brother or sister, you don't forsake that devotion to your success.

Many of you are looking forward to the postgraduation party. Trust me. I am, too. Lainie and I are hanging around here all day just for that reason. But before you run off to crack beers with your buddies and drink good-bye to friends... You look Momma and Daddy square in those tearstained eyes and you tell them, "Thank you." I wish I could go back. I'd do it different. I lost my folks too damn young. And I was too damn selfish to take the time to sit with my momma and detail my graduation. She deserved that. She couldn't be there that day. She was real sick. And I should've taken that day to her. Too selfish. Don't be selfish today. Be selfless. Share this with your family. Trust me, you'll look back and be glad you did.

Everyone who's anyone had someone who believed. I have more than I can possibly name. My parents believed. Nothing I ever aspired to do was scoffed at. It was championed. I work every day to be that champion for others, just like folks were for me.

I'll leave you with this ... have passion

Passion exceeds all traits. Passion wins. Always. You'll meet people who are more talented. You'll meet people with better opportunities. You'll meet people who are smarter and more attractive. Heaven knows I do every day.

But I've never met anyone with greater passion or greater loyalty than me. It's an intangible that can't be taught. If you show up with it, you'll impact people well. And in this life, if you impact people well ... you win.

I was in the gym training the other day ... A nice lady walked up to me and said you're doing so much at ESPN and you're so young. What could possibly be your goal?

Be the best father and husband I can possibly be.

Strive to ensure my children don't know my job is unique.

Be defined by my character and kindness as a man, not my title.

Be the best friend to every friend.

And as it pertains to the job, kick every single ass in my path.

May you guys kick every ass in your path.

Acknowledgments

There are too many people to thank for this book. To my parents, for your love and guidance. In the years since you left us, I've gained perspective about your influence on my life. I miss you every day and cannot wait to see you again.

Most important, Lainie, for your unconditional love, patience, belief in me, tolerance of my shortcomings and mistakes and loving me anyway, for championing my victories and helping me prioritize my failures, for your loyalty and daily acceptance of this crazy ride. I can't imagine doing this life without you.

Cambron, Mia, and Vivian for sharing your daddy with so many others, all the time, and for teaching me daily how to be better. No one inspires me like you three inspire me. You are so beautiful. Mommy and Daddy love you more than anything in the world.

To my sister, Stacy, thank you for always being so enthusiastic about my experiences. I love you and I'm very proud of you. Mom and Dad are, too.

To my extended family, especially Lainie's parents, Don and Sally Cocozza, thank you for embracing an ol' country boy and helping fill an irreplaceable void when my parents died, by loving me like they did. To the outlaws: Don, Farrah, Mike, Brooke, Shaun, Lia, Bethy, Matt, and Andi, thank you for loving me like a brother. To my aunt Becky and my cousins Jim Ed and Rich Wills, and Emily Stewart, I appreciate your support so much.

Thank you so much to the folks at Creative Artists Agency who guide my career, namely my day-to-day representatives, who are not only my agents but also great friends and trusted advisers. Matt Kramer, David Koonin, and David Larabell, your friend-ships and unabashed willingness to fight like hell for me is appre-ciated beyond description. Thank you.

To Sean Desmond, Rachel Kambury, and everyone at Twelve, thank you so much for the opportunity to write this piece. You made a dream come true for a small-town boy with big dreams.

I have an amazing network of friends that are too many to name here. But I must thank a few: First, my brother, Eric Church, for taking the time (during an exhausting tour, no less) to pen such a humbling foreword for this book—it made me belly-laugh and ugly-cry—and for teaching me to be unwavering in attacking my passions.

To my ESPN family, thank you for patiently and deftly teach-ing me television, and supporting my approach to storytelling. Countless talented ESPN executives, producers, editors, camera operators, and audio technicians contributed to the stories in this book. Thank you so much for sharing your talent, vision, leader-ship, and friendship.

To my friends, all of whom helped shape the man I am today, thank you for walking alongside me through various important, vulnerable stages of my personal growth.

Thank you to all my brothers from back home in Virginia. That church-basement bunch and my football teammates. And to the Narrows contingent: One of the great joys of my life is how we turned schoolboy sports hatred into adult brotherhood. It taught me a lot.

I rarely see y'all back home. But please know I feel your support every day.

Go Spartans.

Speaking of the Spartans, thanks are due to longtime *Roanoke Times* preps reporter and columnist Ray Cox, who covered many of my games at Giles High School and who hired me when I was a student at Radford. Ray took a chance on me and taught me how to write. And he was the first person to believe I could.

To the countless athletes, entertainers, and celebrities I've been so fortunate to profile or cover, thank you for your time, candor, and insight. Without you there would be no reason for this book. I am indebted to all of you. You breathed life into these pages and into my dreams to become an author.

Lastly, I'd like to thank the believers. To the readers, viewers, friends, and fans who have supported me for so long, and shown overwhelming kindness: You're the middle finger in my fist, unafraid to hunker down and fight when I need it, unafraid to extend yourselves on my behalf. Thank you.

About the Author

Marty Smith is a reporter for ESPN who covers a wide variety of sports and events for the Worldwide Leader in Sports, including college football and basketball, the NBA, NFL, PGA, and horse racing. He lives in Cornelius, North Carolina, with his wife, Lainie, and three children, Cambron, Mia, and Vivian.